Loving and Living with Animals

Six months in the life of Munlochy Animal Aid

Iona Nicol MBE

Bassman Books

Published by Bassman Books, Burnside Cottage,
Newhall, Balblair, Dingwall, IV7 8LT

First published in 2020

A catalogue record for this book is available from the
British Library

ISBN 978-0-9956440-5-2

Printed by Big Sky, The Press Building,
305 The Park, Findhorn, Forres, IV36 3TE

Layout and design by Russell Turner
www.russellturner.org
Set in Palatino 11/13pt

This book is dedicated to my sister Alexis and my friend Joan Anderson, both of whom passed away whilst it was being written

Introduction

Munlochy Animal Aid (MAA), a registered charity, is situated on the Black Isle, just north of Inverness. My family began rescuing and caring for unwanted, abandoned and stray animals on this site over 40 years ago. The history of MAA was the subject of my first book, *Folk We've Met*, published by Bassman Books in 2019. That book sold very quickly, people commenting on how interesting it was, especially to discover all the work that went on behind the scenes. And so, I decided to offer readers an account of life at MAA, week by week, over a period of six months.

There is no such thing as a typical day. It is frequently chaotic, sometimes sad, but often hilarious. The rituals of feeding, cleaning, going to the vet, and buying foodstuff can be exhausting, but no matter what else is going on these routine tasks have to be undertaken every day of the year. These rituals can be especially tiring when we have a lot of young creatures needing hand rearing, since no sooner have you finished than you have to start again. But life at MAA is never boring. Every day there is something different going on and the unexpected is to be expected, so I hope this book provides the reader with a true flavour of our work.

MAA occupies a range of buildings, barns, sheds, shelters, woods and fields. Over the past 42 years, the centre has grown to its present size. My family are still heavily involved but we now have two full-time and two part-time staff working mainly in the kennel block, along with a team of twenty or so volunteers. Between June 2018 and June 2019 we rehomed 458 animals including 345 dogs and 84 cats so we have plenty to keep us busy.

Iona Nicol MBE
December 2019

Week 1

It may be the first week of June 2019 but is it really summer? We have had rain, sometimes torrential, every day and humans and animals alike are feeling distinctly damp. The car park beside the kennel block looks like a pond and the fields and woods are sodden. Even the forty-three sheep, and especially the six goats, are looking fed up. The pigs do not seem to be too concerned, cosying up in their arcs when it gets too much, and the multitude of chickens, geese and ducks quite like it since it brings worms to the surface. Every animal here has the opportunity to get into some building out of the rain if it wishes, regardless of whether they are dogs, cats, or horses. I have promised them all that we will see the sun again, but when I cannot guarantee.

It is so cold and wet at the moment that our loyal dog walkers plod along the road in their waterproofs, boots and winter bonnets, whilst the more thin-skinned dogs are also kitted out in raincoats. We have been really short of dog walkers each day this week due to various holidays and injuries so it has meant a lot of extra walking for me, my husband, Graham, and the kennel staff. Some dogs really dislike being wet, but most tolerate it if it means they can get a nice bit of exercise and a good sniff, but some, especially Labradors, relish a good soaking. The situation was eased on Saturday when, as part of their commitment to community involvement, a group of staff from a big company in Inverness arrived to join our volunteers for the day. They were great fun, livening up the place despite the weather and they walked a lot of dogs that day.

We have just bought a couple of second-hand barns which Graham and two pals dismantled on the original site and brought back here with the intention of getting them up as quickly as possible. We have needed another barn for a long time because most of our machinery is second-hand and very elderly, so it needs to get some protection from the elements if it is to survive. With a bit of work, we can make the 'new' barns watertight, create a hayloft and section off somewhere cosy for some of the animals to use. Our intention was to have it up and, since we have already bought a load of cheap paint, we would ask our next team of Saturday helpers from the Inverness company to paint it for us. However, the weather has conspired against us and it will not be up in time for next weekend when they arrive. Never mind, they can paint the old sheds for us and, of course, walk some more dogs if they feel inclined!

Most of the dogs that end up at MAA find homes reasonably quickly. We need this to happen otherwise we would run out of kennel space. However, we currently have quite a few dogs that are proving slow to rehome, some because they are elderly and folk worry about veterinary bills. Three of these dogs came in when their owners died, so they are not dogs with particular 'problems'. Bobby is a lovely, rather portly, old Labrador/cross. Biggie is not that big but she probably has some German Shepherd somewhere in her genes and her constant companion, who she came in with, is a Border Collie called Brindle, although she is actually black and white. I would like to rehome them together since they really dislike being separated, even on walks.

I would also like to find a home together for two middle-aged long-staying male Lurchers, Sting and Speedy. They have had lit- tle or no training in their original home and Speedy is particularly reactive to strange dogs. This week they may have caught the eye of a lady who has experience of the breed and appreciates that these two have to stay on their leads. With their backgrounds it would be impossible to take the risk of them chasing anything that moved quicker than a snail. I am hoping she comes back and so are they.

We also have a couple of younger long-stay dogs awaiting homes. One is a huge and very healthy Anatolian Shepherd Dog from Spain. The breed is kept to guard livestock from wolves. Rocky is extremely handsome, strong and very boisterous. He real- ly is not able to settle into a normal home environment because we

2

Rocky

have tried to rehome him, each time without success, despite it being with experienced dog owners. Rocky finds it hard to do the socialising stuff that is normally required of a dog in a home. He really needs to live outdoors in a nice heated kennel within a big dog run. He loves long walks and a couple of our dog walkers have really taken to him and so he has some degree of continuity in this respect. I am hopeful that someone will come along who has the space and experience to manage this type of dog and who will take seriously his issues because his breeding and background are not his fault.

And then there is Cooper, a deaf, mainly white Border Collie that is a young, energetic, excitable dog. He is very pretty and a lot of people show an interest in him but, so far, nobody has been able to provide the level of commitment that he needs. But, we live in hope that all our longer stay residents will find homes in the weeks to come. All I can say is 'Watch this space!'

Other dogs come and go and we have a steady flow through the kennel block. We are always receiving strays from the dog wardens, the police or members of the public. Quite often, they are reunited with their owners the same day. I was overjoyed to see one dog brought in by the warden who, along with various other folk, had been trying to catch this particular dog, on and off, for almost a year. It had been seen wandering so often in a really busy part of the city of Inverness that we had all begun to think it was abandoned and just surviving on its wits. However, it turned out to have an owner who arrived at the kennel to reclaim it, denying completely that the dog had ever been roaming. At least now we all know who owns it and where they live, so maybe greater efforts will be made to stop it leaving its home alone.

Some dogs come in when they are signed over to MAA when their owners can, for a variety of reasons, no longer keep them. This week, these included a lovely-natured Collie called Tweed who is just not the least bit interested in working, preferring cuddles and play, so he should not be with us too long. Our other new admission is a lovely wee dog who we were warned had an unfortunate 'attitude problem'. Though small and cute-looking, he has since proved his 'attitude problem' but we have taken the opportunity to get him groomed, his ears cleaned, his claws trimmed, his teeth looked at and his anal glands emptied, all in an effort to make him more comfortable and, perhaps, amenable. He loves being taken out for a walk and doing what he wants to do but otherwise he just sits looking grumpy, hence his nickname of 'Grumpy'. We will have to give him time and see if a suitable owner comes along. But, everything is affected by the weather, including the number of people visiting the kennel, so there has been no rehoming and, consequently, we are short of kennel space.

We have just taken delivery of another five feral cats to add to the fifty or so that we already have. Our colony of feral cats live in two huge sheds with outside access to a playground of trees and 'toys' that Graham makes for them to climb on, in, down and around. Feral cats frequently live an awful life in the wild, especially when they get ill or old and there is no human being to help

Cooper

them, and so we do not send them back to this fate. These five had been living, along with a number of other cats, in less than ideal conditions and came to us when the person caring for them passed away. Surprisingly, all five are in very good condition. Like all our ferals, we have had them neutered, health-checked and vaccinated, but we are caring for them in one of the smaller sheds that has access to an outside area but is away from the other feral cat buildings. I am hopeful, given the fact that they have been used to a human being, that they may be suitable, eventually, for rehoming. They are already showing signs of calming down around Graham and me. They are even accepting a gentle touch now and then, but only time will tell. If we decide they should remain here then we will very gradually introduce them into one of the existing feral groups. Initially, they will be put into the kitchen area where they can see the other cats and they can see them, but not mix. The good

A lovely pair of feral cats

thing is that they are already used to living in a bigger colony of cats and there is so much space both inside the cat barns and outside that they can be as sociable as they want to be or not be sociable at all.

Every week we get folk ringing up or calling in asking for help of one sort or another. Some of the requests for help can be a little bit annoying. The week started with a telephone call at 1am. The chap on the phone demanded that I go to a particular location, many miles away, to get his dog. He explained that he had been forced, at short notice, to leave his accommodation by his partner but the dog was microchipped to him, so it was his and he wanted it.

'So,' he shouted, 'if you call yourself a dog-lover you will get yourself up there now and get my dog!'

My response was an equally emphatic refusal to get involved in this. There followed a good bit of shouting and swearing from this caller until both Graham and I were fully wide awake. Topsy, our cat that sleeps on our bed, slept peacefully through all this but we did not get back to sleep until around 3am. We were woken again at 6.20am by another telephone call, this time from a man who was so drunk he could hardly speak. The gist of what he was slurring was that he had lost his dog. I tried to get some details but much of it was unintelligible. Not much point in trying to get some more shut-eye. Fortunately, an hour later he rang back to say he had found his dog and all was well.

On Tuesday, a man who had bought a ten-week-old pedigree puppy for £600 on Sunday night asked if we were prepared to vaccinate it. I pointed out that it should already have had vaccinations and did he really think it was reasonable to ask a small charity to pay for these when he could afford the £600. He then asked if we were not prepared to do it, how was he supposed to get it vaccinated and where? I suggested a vet! Only the week before we had a lady on the telephone after she had paid £350 to a charity who bring in dogs from overseas. She had believed the dog she took would already have been neutered and vaccinated but this was apparently not the case and she really did not have the money. Given the circumstances she described I agreed to help with some of the funding but it makes me very cross when people are not made aware of the kind of commitment they are embarking upon.

I felt so sorry for a gentleman who arrived clearly upset. He had been living with an indoor cat for years when, suddenly, it had shot out when the door was opened. The man had taken steps to entice it back by leaving tasty food out, which it ignored, and eventually resorting to a cat-trap. His cat was seen regularly in the immediate vicinity of his home and he was worried that it just could not find the right house. Neither he nor his wife had been sleeping at night, getting up at all hours to look out of the window. House cats get very spooked when they find themselves out in the big wide world and can take some time to recover themselves enough to calm down and return. I did tell him about the wonders of a fish supper since most animals cannot resist the smell of it and we have used it ourselves when we have been having difficulty capturing a stray. Fortunately, his cat returned unharmed but hungry.

I am just in the process of completing our annual return to the Office of the Scottish Charity Commissioner. I have to list all the different animals that came into our care and their eventual destination, including those that passed away or are remaining with us for their natural lives. The financial accounts are always sobering since we run at a loss. Averaged out, it now costs between £3,000 and £3,500 each week to run this establishment. Last year our deficit was £11,000 but the year before it was nearer to £50,000. Last year our donations were up by £12,000 and we managed to shed £9,000 from our food bills. Our income from fundraising was down by £4,000 and we spent £32,000 on veterinary fees. And that is what it is like: some up and some down each year, which does not help with forward planning. No matter what else has to be done, I have to complete the accounts by the end of June each year, so the dining table is covered in bits of paper, bank statements, receipts etc. I just wish the phone would stop ringing long enough for me to do it and our cats would stop shuffling the papers as they stalk around the table.

Week 2

Within our own home, our clan of dogs and cats have been getting accustomed to the new puppy, a very lively, enthusiastic German Shepherd that was handed in by her first owners. She has the biggest paws you have ever seen and little control over where they go! We have had some sad times this year with a couple of our beloved dogs and cats having to be put to sleep, so this new arrival is a joy. She has, however, had to learn her place within the home and is still misbehaving with one of the cats and annoying one of the older Collies. She has stopped bullying our elderly, visually impaired Jack Russell, so progress is being made. We have called her Tara, after one of the dogs that were put to sleep earlier in the year, in the hope that she will have a similar temperament. New Tara rampages around, knocking over ornaments, cushions and anything else that happens to get in her way. She loves people and I am hopeful that, once she calms down a bit, she might end up being able to accompany me on talks that I give to various organisations.

Earlier this year, Gertie our old pig died and Pippa, her companion, was devastated. Pippa was clearly depressed, grieving and off her food, which was unheard of since she is particularly keen on it. She even went off her favourite biscuit treat! I put an advert in a local newspaper saying that we were looking for a pig as companion to Pippa. On the same morning that the paper went into circulation we got an offer of not one but two pigs from the same home. Moira and Susan pig needed to be rehomed together and so we took them both. They were very nervous when they were introduced to Pippa, who is much bigger than they are. In fact, Pippa is a huge pig and when she towered over them they must have thought she was a monster. Pippa showed no aggression towards them and within a couple of days all three were eating happily and now sleep, by choice, in the same arc. Moira and Susan are really sweet-natured and love attention from humans, so we now have three happy porkers on site. They have a lovely home in amongst trees which, should we ever get strong sunlight, will provide some protection for their skin. It also provides shelter from the wind and so they are in piggy clover.

A man telephoned one day this week to say the SSPCA had recommended he phone us because they said we would take on a difficult dog. He arrived with the dog and signed it over to us so that it could be rehomed. However, he made it clear that the dog really did have issues, having apparently killed other animals and attacked a person. He explained that it had come from the south where it had been bred for fighting. It was microchipped but still registered to the original owner because the new owner had never updated its details. This is not uncommon and makes rehoming strays very difficult.

The dog was fine with us when it was inside the kennels, although it did look very subdued; it was a very different picture when it was outside. It was apparent to me that if this dog got off the lead it would be a killing machine! Shortly after, we had a couple in viewing dogs for a potential rehome and this was the one they decided they wanted to offer a home to. I explained that this dog was not yet ready for rehoming. Quite sensibly, they came back a couple of times to see the dog but because of its nature I explained that I would not be letting it go out for quite a long time yet. They were not the least bit interested in any other dog.

We have no idea how, but somehow, the man who signed the dog over to us found out that this couple were interested in rehoming what he clearly still saw as 'his dog', despite having signed it over. He telephoned one evening whilst we were having a meal and was raging about me selling his dog. I explained, when I could get a word in, that I had never sold a dog in my life and did not plan to start now and the dog in question was going nowhere until we were sure of its behaviour. In his anger, he threatened to come to the house and to raid the kennels, at which point Graham, who was sitting at the table listening to the abuse I was taking, took the telephone and, in very expressive language, explained that this

Pippa Pig

was not the way to carry on. When Graham wants to make a point he really does, and the caller slammed the phone down.

We had no choice but to inform the police because the safety of a number of animals resident here was being threatened. The police visited him and told him to calm down and stay away from MAA. He explained that he just wanted his dog back. Once a dog has been signed over we are not obliged to hand it back and I was concerned about letting the dog go back to him, more for the safety of other animals since, as I said, we had a pretty good idea as to what it was capable of. But, at the same time, I was not sure there was anything to be gained by not letting him have it back since he clearly cared and it would be in kennels with us most likely for a very long time with no guarantee that it would be a happy ending. In the end, I decided to let him have it back and when he came to collect it he was calm and controlled and clearly just wanted to take his dog. It left me feeling very unsure about whether I should or should not have done this.

I later discovered, piecing together various bits of information, that the chap had taken his dog to a vet, had it put to sleep and it was now at rest, buried in his garden. I actually felt that this was the best outcome for the dog since it was definitely difficult to manage and dangerous in its present state. It was sad because the dog had never had the kind of life most dogs enjoy within a home environment, out enjoying walks and meeting other animals. The dog's breeding and early upbringing had sealed his fate.

We were very disappointed about the rehoming of our two long-stay Lurchers, Sting and Speedy. The couple who were going to rehome them had experience of sight hounds and were used to the characteristics of the breed, so it appeared to be a match made in heaven. However, they took them home one day and returned them the next. Apparently, they had done their business around the house and one of them had managed to open all the doors, so the couple felt they could not cope with this pair. We knew they would be challenging, and this was explained, but when you rehome a dog, especially after it has been in kennels for a long time, you need to give it at least seven to ten days to adjust and set-tle into the new environment. We also suspect that, out of kind-ness, they may have over-indulged the skinny-looking pair with the resultant upset to their digestive systems since they have never made a mess here in their kennel.

One of the biggest mistakes people make when taking a dog from kennels is thinking that now is the time to make up for its past and to give it everything you think it has missed out on. This may be in relation to food, affection or just letting it do what it wants and not giving it a row. In the kennels, dogs have been given the right amount of a particular type of food and any change in diet should be introduced gradually. In fact, the first week to ten days is when you should be the firmest and set the boundaries so that the animal knows what is acceptable in its new home. Of course, you give plenty of love but do not overwhelm it with cud-dles and kisses. We all like cuddles and kisses but maybe not on the first date! My advice is just to let the animal settle in and you will be rewarded with a long-lasting relationship.

Judy at 17, or maybe older

The good news this week was that Grumpy, the wee chap with an 'attitude problem', has gone to a new home and will be called Harvey. The new owner is someone I am well acquainted with and so we are working together to manage Grumpy's attitude. The new owner seems to have taken my advice on board and, so far, there have been no unpleasant incidents. He is a nice wee dog that has just been used to getting his own way and doing whatever he wants, when he wants to do it. It is a similar situation to Judy, our own Jack Russell. Judy was taken into our home after she had spent many months in the kennels and was unlikely to get rehomed due to her tendency to snap under certain circumstances. She is an old lady and going blind, so Graham and I know what we can and cannot do with Judy and we all rub along nicely. She can be very affectionate when she feels like it!

Week 3

We had three sets of volunteers out fundraising over the weekend. One managed to sell more of my first book *Folk We've Met: The Story of Munlochy Animal Aid* along with our fete raffle tickets. Another volunteer who sells second-hand leads, beds, toys, bowls etc under the name of *Bella's Bargains* attended a three-day event held on the Black Isle Showground and raised the amazing sum of £1,332. Two poor souls took six crates of second-hand books to sell at a village hall table top sale and raised £11.50, with great difficulty. Most of the people looking through the books on display were avid readers but said they already had a pile of books beside their bed waiting to be read. They did, however, manage to sell a book to a man who said he had never read a book in his life. He turned to a friend and exclaimed in astonishment, 'She's just sold me a book for 50p!' Rather than buying books, some people were bringing their own unwanted books for the stall because they had heard we were having a bookstall. So, our volunteers came back with £11.50 and more books than they went with! Shortly after this, we received a donation of almost 2,000 children's books following an appeal for unwanted books which we can sell on our bookstall. The couple who had, for years, managed our book stall near the checkouts of Inverness Co-operative store wanted to retire and we were very fortunate in getting a volunteer to take it on. We now have a shed dedicated solely to storing second-hand books and our volunteer, Lesley, has got them organised in different genres and is even managing to sell some on the internet. Fifty pence a book does not sound like much but, when every penny counts, it all makes a difference

We had a wonderful opportunity this week when we received a letter from a firm of solicitors on the south coast of England. The letter asked if we wanted to apply for a grant from the Edna Smylie Memorial Fund which they administer along with a board of trustees. Normally, they only make grants available within England and Wales, so we have no idea how they heard about our small charity in the Highlands of Scotland. One of my many tasks for next week is to complete the grant application form asking for the money to purchase a second-hand tractor which we desperately need. If we get our 'new' barn put up, we can keep it tucked up out of the elements.

Very few people realise that this charity provides as much support as it can for human beings as well as animals. This does not mean that we just dish out money to anyone who asks but, depending upon the circumstances, we will sometimes help with neutering fees or other veterinary expenses which we pay direct to the vet and we offer free microchipping. We have food donation boxes in some of the supermarkets and although the majority of the donations in these will be used within MAA, what is left goes into food banks accessed by families in need. Struggling to feed yourself, your children and your pet is a not infrequent occurrence these days.

I received a call from a man who had fallen on hard times and his call to Munlochy Animal Aid was to ask if we could provide some food for his dog because he had used up everything he had. He explained that there was now no food and no money. Obviously, when we get a call like this I ask various questions and I have been doing this job for so long that I am pretty good at differentiating the genuine from the not so genuine! One of my questions was to ask whether he had food for himself and his response was, 'If I had any food, do you not think I would have given it to the dog?' I took his name and address and later that day Graham and I went along with a big bag of dog food. Before we left home, I raided our own cupboards taking out bread, butter, jam, milk and a couple of other bits and pieces. When we got to his address we were greeted by a happy, if hungry, dog that carried around a big ball. The man looked very grey and said he was not long out of hospital. I got a chance to see inside his cupboards and they were virtually empty. It was exceptionally cold. When we left, we arranged for £20, from our own money rather than the charity's money, to go onto his electricity key. I hope he has managed to sort himself out with the help of social services but, of course, I could not contact them on his behalf to say they needed to get help to this man because of privacy laws.

One caller this week said her dog needed an amputation after an accident. She said that seagulls were nesting near her home and had been swooping down over her garden, annoying the dog. This resulted in him jumping up to try to catch them. However, he misjudged his jump and fell back down to earth with a crash, sustaining a broken leg in the process. The leg was so badly broken that it could not be mended and required amputation. The owner was on a limited income and this was an unexpected expense which she could not fully fund. On this occasion, we agreed to part fund, sending the money direct to the vet who was going to carry out the operation. People appeal to MAA because, at the moment, there is nowhere else to go in the Highlands.

We have all heard folk say that you should not have a pet if you cannot afford to keep it and to anticipate veterinary bills. But someone's circumstances can change overnight and a pet is a family member. Some folk are forgoing their own wellbeing in order to keep their pet. Today, many people we come across are existing on very limited resources whether they are elderly, disabled, unemployed or homeless and one of the few joys in their life may be their pet. Some animals are signed over to us under these circumstances which are always a very sad occasion for the owner, the pet and for us.

This week, we have seventeen horses in our fields. I was never going to take any more when we had sixteen but we got a call asking us to take another horse. I asked a couple of volunteers to come with me to see this horse since they knew a lot about horses. Information given to us over the phone suggested there was a 50:50 chance that we would need to bring the horse back here. The folk who had it had taken the horse in and had nowhere suitable for it. As a result, they had tied it to a tree with no water and no food and because it had gone round and round the tree it was now on a short rope staring straight into the tree. When we knocked at the door various people emerged, along with a Lurcher who clearly was not friendly. I am no athlete, but I cleared a fence that day

One very contented horse

with this dog in hot pursuit. When it could not get me or my companions it sunk its teeth into the thigh of a young man who lived in the house, much to the amusement of the other occupants. We took the horse, needless to say.

Horses are really expensive to keep even though Graham does the haymaking so that we don't have to buy in any hay. We are producing around £7,000 of hay each year and our old tractor is on its last legs. Everyone is doing haymaking around the same time and so we cannot just borrow a tractor since they are all in use. We have bought a rake and a baler and Graham spends hours working alone doing this.

A lot of people have no idea what hard work horses are. There is always something needing to be done, whether it is unfreezing their water early on a winter's morning, cleaning their stables, rugging up, checking for physical problems or getting their hooves trimmed. Our horses do not need to be shod because they are never out of their fields but their feet have to be trimmed every few weeks. My niece is so confident with horses and always has been since she was a little girl and, thankfully, she has taken over dealing with the horses. They have a number of shelters in their fields so that they can choose when to go in and out and which other horses they want to be with and which they want to avoid.

When we have a domestic cat handed over, it is usually quickly rehomed. Fortunately, there are not so many kittens around these days so folk can have difficulty getting a cat. Cats are generally much more timid than dogs and having members of the public viewing the cattery could be upsetting to them, so we do not allow access. When someone makes an enquiry for a cat, we ask a lot of questions. I find out where they live; who shares the home; whether they have had cats before; and how near they are to a road. It is not unusual to have someone say that they have had their four previous cats run over outside their house. No – I am not providing them with number five! We try to narrow down what it is they are looking for. For example, are they looking for long or short hair; are they fussy about colour; male or female etc. Once we are sure they can provide a safe and loving home for a cat we bring the cat out to them and, nine times out of ten, we have matched it to their needs and cat and new owner are happy. Even when we are inundated with cats needing homes we are very fussy about where they are going to. We offer a cat boarding service and have done for a number of years, so some of our rehomed cats come back to us for their annual holiday!

One of our own cats, Topsy, was found as a tiny kitten of four weeks beside a busy road. She needed to go into our makeshift incubator that is based on an old fish tank. We had to provide a lot of support for her in the early months. Having spent so much time with her we found we could not offer her up for rehoming and so she joined our tribe. Poor Topsy suffers from feline stomatitis which means that the cat's own immune system attacks the oral tissues and is very painful. Poor Topsy had already lost a number of teeth and was off to the vet again this week to have eleven teeth removed. She is very small and was so poorly after the operation that we had to take her back on Sunday to the vet for emergency treatment. However, Topsy is fine now and enjoying a nice soft diet but insisting on having her six Dreamies (a hard, crunchy cat

Topsy the diva

treat) from me and six from Graham every morning. She must be gumming them!

Remember Tweed, the lovely Border Collie who wanted play not work and was handed over two weeks ago? Tweed has got a wonderful home with a local couple who have recently lost a much loved, elderly Border Collie. Tweed is apparently settling in with no trouble at all and is definitely staying with them for the rest of his life.

Week 4

A few weeks ago, we received fourteen three-week-old ducklings from a man who feeds and cares for wild birds in Nairn. He was going into hospital for a short while but he felt the ducklings were not safe since a number had been killed by loose dogs. These thrived with us, staying in a safe enclosure with a hose running so they could paddle about to their heart's content. This week, they have reached seven weeks old and six of them have gone to a couple of volunteers who live near the canal outside Inverness. Whilst they are free to come and go and swim on the canal with all the other ducks that this couple care for, they return for food every day. When Graham delivered these six ducklings they went straight into the garden and other ducks came in to have a look at the new arrivals. Then one of the ducklings discovered he could squeeze out under the gate so the gate was opened to allow all of them to be on the other side. Suddenly, they saw the great expanse of water in the canal and all six jumped into it, had a swim and then climbed out again and back into the garden for the next meal. The remaining ducklings are going back to Nairn now their guardian has returned.

We have just taken delivery of twelve battery hens brought to us by the Hen Rescue Society. They collected them from an enormous establishment down in the Borders and if they had not rescued them they would just have been killed. Unfortunately, four of them had to be put down because they were in a hellish state. They were all almost featherless and their back ends were in a dreadful state including two with major prolapses. They lay huge eggs, more like goose eggs but are such tiny fragile birds. They came from those horrible living conditions to all this freedom with lovely grass, fresh air and worms and if they could have shouted 'wow' when they saw it they would. We give them things like cider vinegar in their water, vitamins and tonics and gradually their feathers will come back. They will be wandering freely with all our other chickens and quickly learn where they can and cannot go. At least the rest of their lives will be happier.

Some dogs bark a lot when they are in kennels. There is always so much going on and once one starts barking then, one by one, the others join in. One Staffordshire Bull Terrier, Sally, was a barking ring leader and was driving the kennel staff mad. Much to their relief, she has been rehomed this week to a lovely family who walked her, fell in love with her and passed the home inspection. She does not bark if she is getting attention or is out for a walk, so let us hope that she does not bark so much in a normal home environment. However, someone has taken over the role of 'barking chorus leader'!

Hunter has returned to MAA and can he bark! He is a Beagle/cross and he was a challenge when we rehomed him eighteen months ago. The arrangements were not ideal but we thought there was a reasonably good chance that he would have found his forever home, so it was worth giving it a try. Sometimes, there are circumstances that mean the match between dog and potential new home are not totally ideal but so long as there is a good chance of success it is sometimes worth it, especially if it is the only chance of a home that the dog has been offered. He had been seen out on walks with his new owners and the reports back were that he looked happy and well-fed, so we were hopeful that everything was working out. But the owner's circumstances have changed now and they just do not want a dog any more, especially this one that pulls on his lead and is generally hard work, having a wilful streak. There are no comments about him being aggressive with other dogs or people and he is an attractive size with an easily managed coat, so he may find another home fairly soon.

When I rehome any dog or cat, I give the potential owner as much information as possible so that they can think through all the issues and how the animal will fit in with their lifestyle. It does nobody any good, neither human nor animal, to have to return an animal and is a sad occasion for all concerned.

This week we are looking after a lovely Spaniel called Tess. Tess is on holiday while her owner goes for a break. The reason we have Tess is because the last time the owner went on holiday she put Tess into a boarding kennels from where she promptly went missing. When the owner returned from holiday to collect her, she was told the dog had got out and, although they had seen her up on the hills, there seemed to have been very little done to recapture her. The owner contacted the dog warden who contacted us to see if she could borrow the dog trap. This trap is very heavy and so I said that Graham and I would go up into the hills with the trap.

The first time we went up that hill we took one of our own dogs with us because a dog can attract another dog, but there was no sign of Tess. We went up again after having something to eat but still no sign of the dog. The only thing to do was to take the trap up and set it. However, if we set the trap someone has to be monitoring it regularly and so we organised some local folk to keep watch. One family were close enough to use binoculars to keep checking the box. Graham and I went back the next day, once in the morning and again in the evening. It wasn't until that evening visit that we spotted the dog. We set the trap with the smelliest food we could get and then walked around dropping bits of food in a sort of trail. We came away and went back three hours later and Tess was in the box. She was, apparently, always a very timid dog but she was really very frightened by her experience. We contacted the owner and arranged a meeting point. She was overjoyed but she said she would never go away again because she just could not trust a kennel not to lose her dog. Of course, we now had to go back up the hill and get our cage back, so we were well exercised that day and it was about a thirty-mile drive each time back and forth from here to that hill. I remember telling the owner that if she ever wanted to go away I would take the dog for its holiday. We never 'board' dogs because we are not a boarding kennels but we do sometimes take in a dog that we have had contact with in the past if the owner cannot find a suitable kennel. Tess will go home next week to a relieved owner.

Over in Garve, a village some miles from here, there had been a cat straying for quite a while and eventually someone we know managed to get it into their porch. The first thing we did when they brought it to us was to check if it had a microchip and it did.

I telephoned the owners in Forres, a village in completely the opposite direction, and asked if they were missing a cat. The chap said their cat had been gone for a month and they had given up hope of getting it back, taking all its stuff to the vet so that someone else could use it. He was overjoyed to hear that we had his cat and set off to collect it straight away. The cat, which was a good big, healthy cat to start with, was not in a bad condition after the month straying and had probably been catching mice and birds. We guessed it might have got into a delivery van since Forres to Garve is a considerable distance.

It reminded me of one of our cats, Barney, who was a home loving cat who would respond to my whistle. On this particular day, he just did not come when I called. Then we got a call from the lorry driver who had been with us that morning delivering animal food. When he arrived outside Boots shop in Dingwall, Barney jumped down off his spare wheel and took himself into the shop. He was captured and the lorry driver took him with him to his next delivery which was to a kennels over Kirkhill way where we met him to collect Barney. I was crying the entire journey there and back because I kept thinking about what might have happened to him sitting on that wheel. So, we will never know how a cat got from Forres to Garve but anything is possible.

Tara, our own GSD puppy, continues to be too rough and boisterous for one of our own Border Collies called Moss but when she tries it on with the other one, Scampy, he soon sends her packing with a snarl. She is only wanting to play and they are both willing to accommodate her until it all becomes a bit too much and they just want her to go an lie down. At nearly eight months old she is dreadfully clumsy but with paws that size it is difficult not to be. The other evening, Graham and I were watching something on television, gratefully putting our feet up and Graham treating himself to a rum and coke. The doorbell rang and Graham went to answer it, so Tara nipped into the armchair he had vacated. It was then that she spotted his glass on the coffee table and proceeded to help herself to a slurp before I could retrieve it. It was clearly to her taste but, fortunately, she only got a little and with no adverse effects.

Tara is a really busy puppy from morning to night and so when she does go to her bed, she sleeps really deeply and humans, cats and dogs all breathe a sigh of relief. We take her everywhere we can so that she has a wide range of experiences and she travels well in the car. If we visit someone else's house she settles down fairly quickly after exploring to start with, just to see if there is any food around. Of course, I could never take her anywhere that there was a table full of food since she would be sure it was all for her! Her exploration includes climbing the stairs, but she cannot work out how she can get down those same stairs and has to be carried down.

Last weekend we went to Loch Carron, setting up a gazebo to offer free microchipping. At last, we had a gorgeous, sunny, June day and I said to Graham that we must take the opportunity to let Tara go into the loch because she has not had the chance to go swimming yet. On the way home we stopped where there was a fairly narrow inlet to let her paddle but she was very wary. I threw a stone into the water thinking she would want to chase it, but when it plopped into the water she nearly jumped out of her skin. She still would not go further into the water, so Graham went over to the other side of the inlet and called her until she splashed her way across to him. I called her from my side but she was very wary of re-crossing the water. I waded in, called her and pretended to run away and that was it – she bounded clumsily around in the water, absolutely loving it. It was not deep enough for her to have to swim but at least she had learned to enjoy water on a hot day.

There are two boys who want to work here on their Duke of Edinburgh Award scheme. This week I met them at the kennels in order that I might make a judgement as to whether or not they will fit in with our team and the work we do. I believe it is important to meet them face-to-face rather than just talk with them over the telephone. I need to know that they can take instruction and have a realistic idea of what the work involves. I watch their reactions to the sights, sounds and smells of this place. They need to realise that they start at 9am even if it is a Sunday morning, so no long lie-ins! We obviously have insurance here but I need to know that they are sensible enough not to do anything that could put them-selves or others at risk and these two met the bill. They will join us for two or three hours on a Saturday or Sunday, working mainly

Two lovely Borders

around the kennels. Some of those who choose MAA for their work experience option do it just because they like animals but quite a few of these youngsters end up working in occupations where they are dealing with animals. Some end up qualifying as vets or veterinary nurses and a couple of the local vets worked at MAA on Duke of Edinburgh Awards when they were young. These latest lads will start in August and, hopefully, they will thoroughly enjoy the experience.

Graham had to go and pick up some donated meat for the birds of prey. I get Graham to do this because, being a vegetarian myself, I find it really difficult to look at this stuff. He is great at doing the jobs I do not want to do: for instance he has to do the microchipping of puppies and cats because I just cannot stick that great big needle in them. He was able to stop off at the vets and collect calcium tablets for our young German Shepherd Dog, Tara. She is a big, active young dog and will benefit from these for another few months. Then he had to go down the A9 to check on what had been run over because we received a call to say a Labrador puppy was dead at the side of the road. It turned out to be a hare, but that was sad too.

It has been a busy week and there have been days when I have been out of my house from 9am to 3pm without ever getting back to see my own animals. Graham will be in and out of the house throughout the day so they are not left alone but I really long to get back to them. We are so lucky to have the paid staff who work with us because they are so committed and never refuse to do anything, doing everything with good grace. We all work as a team but Graham and I have never taken a wage from the charity so our unpaid jobs do not come with holidays or sick pay and we are on duty twenty-four hours a day, seven days a week, fifty-two weeks in a year, but we love it!

Week 5

If the first week of July is anything to go by, July seems to be going to follow the weather pattern of June – that is, it is very wet. The absence of sun has meant that the chickens do not get their much loved dust bath. The ex-battery hens that joined them are fitting in well and getting their feathers back. All the chickens can wander freely and even saunter up to the kennel block since they are not bothered by the barking. They wander into our garden searching for treats and into the car park, but they know just how far they can go. We have a few cockerels and, although we do not look for homes for the hens, we have rehomed a couple of cockerels so that we can avoid fights. The cockerels we have kept all get along well together and sometimes can be seen sitting in a row along the roof. One of the cockerels was born under the hedge behind our house, so he has been strutting around here from a very young age.

We have a lot of wild birds handed in by members of the public. At the moment, we have a baby seagull that fell from a chimney pot nest in Cromarty. He had no feathers, just a downy covering when he arrived. By this week, he is fully feathered and living in an empty rabbit enclosure with a hutch so he could go in and out as he pleases and, to my surprise, he always goes inside if it is raining. Various seagulls who visit here for their daily feed have wandered over to look at him. If I am generous, I would say they are looking at him with sympathy, but I think they are really eyeing up his bowl of food, which looks more appetising than their meal! When he is ready, we will introduce him gradually to the two seagulls that cannot fly and live here permanently in a fenced-off area during the day. They are shut in a shed at night so that the fox does not get them. When baby seagull feels confident to fly he will take off and what usually happens is he will come back for his daily feed along with the hundreds of other seagulls who land here every morning. We may put a ring on his leg so that people can see he has been around humans and been handled, which may make them more tolerant towards him since folk can be quite nasty to these beautiful birds.

Quite often we have wild animals handed in and we have had wildcats, seals, otters, squirrels goats and foxes, but hedgehogs are always being brought in, especially at the start of winter when they are found in distress because they are too small to hibernate and are starving. But this one was spotted by some kind folk who recognised that something was very wrong with its face. I took it to the vet who said that what looked like an open cut on its face was, in fact, either a tumour or an infected cyst and the kindest thing to do was to put it to sleep. A sad ending but at least the hedgehog was saved from a very nasty, prolonged period of suffering.

The police have been in and out of here all week. They brought in a wee dog that was found, with a ball in his mouth, at the side of the road near Drumsmittal. It was after 10pm by the time we checked for a microchip but found that it had not been registered. I was planning to put him on our Facebook page the next day when the owners rang to ask if a stray had been handed in. Apparently, he had received a shock off an electric fence and bolted as a consequence. By 11.10pm, dog, ball and owners were happily reunited and we could go to bed.

The police also brought in two dogs whose owners had been arrested for drunken behaviour. Usually, these people spend a night in the cells and are released early the next morning. The owner of the first dog contacted us to tell us where we could bring her dog so she and the dog could be reunited! I pointed out, politely, that there was a good bus service from where she was calling, but, failing that, there were taxis, so she would need to come and collect the dog from us. She was very rude but arrived by taxi later the next day and took her dog away with her, without even a 'thank-you'! We had, however, taken the opportunity to tidy the animal up since he was looking a bit neglected.

The second dog, a lovely Husky, had been reported to the police by members of the public who had seen his owner lying drunk in a cemetery all day, but the dog had no access to water and no food. The owner was arrested and this lovely, good-natured dog brought here where I managed to give him a clean-up too and, before the police released the now sober owner from their cells, I got the dog health-checked by a vet. It does have ongoing health issues but I had no choice but to return the dog to its owner. We provided the transport this time because it would have been a long and complicated journey for the older gentleman and really, the Husky could do without that.

As I have said, we need to keep a flow through of dogs in the kennels because space is at a premium. When I rehome a dog, I always tell people that they should try to give the dog a week or so to settle in but, if during the first month they feel they cannot cope, for whatever reason, I will take it back straight away, on the day they telephone. However, when someone has had an animal for some time I expect the owner to telephone me and explain the problems, since we may be able to help. If they feel returning the dog is the best solution then I will give them a time and date when they can bring the animal in. I will always take an animal but, with restricted space, planning is important and I need to have as many vacant pens as possible to accommodate strays brought in. When we run out of kennel space, and the isolation block is full, we have no choice but to put some of the smaller dogs in crates and that is something we avoid if possible.

Unfortunately, on Tuesday, a dog that we had rehomed three years ago, when she was nine months old, was brought back. The story was that the owner was unable to manage her and she is a young, strong dog and had pulled him over a couple of times. Apparently, she has to be walked at times and in places where they are unlikely to meet other dogs or people because of her reactions and she cannot be left home alone, howling to the annoyance of the neighbours. Despite a couple of efforts with professional trainers, this has been going on for three years! Betty was brought to the kennels with no prior contact and the entire family were clearly very distressed, so, under the circumstances, I took this handsome German Shepherd bitch but it meant that we had to do some shuffling around in the kennel to accommodate an unexpected arrival. We were praying that the police would not bring in another stray overnight since we had no space left.

And then, the next day, Wednesday, a lady telephoned to ask if we would take her Lurcher because she was going on holiday on Friday! In other words, we had a day in which to act. We are not, as I told her, a boarding kennel. It was then that she explained she did not want it back and asked if we would take it if she signed it over for rehoming. It was a lovely gentle dog and someone took a fancy to it straight away, passed the home check and it went out over the weekend. We really needed the space because we had heard that the police were bringing in a St Bernard because her owner had been taken into hospital as an emergency and a Border Collie was already on its way in with some kind people who had found it wandering.

Fingers crossed, we may have a vacant kennel soon because Bobby, one of our very happy long-stay oldies, may be getting a home. Bobby, a rather stout gentleman Labrador/cross, adores people. Unfortunately, he is reactive to other dogs so this means we will need to do a careful home check to make sure he will be secure wherever he goes to live. The couple who are interested have looked at him twice, so they seem keen. He came to us when his owner died in tragic circumstances, so he was not brought to MAA because of any behavioural issues and he will make a loving companion for someone.

Our own darling Tara has been getting into trouble again. This time, she decided to lick the paint whilst Graham was painting a big second-hand planter he had bought me. This meant there was paint all down her front as well as on her mouth. When he had repainted where necessary, I planted it up with a wee shrub and some flowers to make it look nice in readiness for the coming annual fete but Graham came in and informed me that I should come and see what she has done to it. Where were my plants, or what were left of them?

Graham and I have had a lot of lively, boisterous dogs like Tara so we are used to the antics. Many years ago, a young couple arrived with two tiny Staffie/Labrador puppies that were one day old. They were minute, fitting easily in the palm of your hand. The mother had experienced difficulty giving birth and they did not have the money to take her to a vet, so she had died. The wee

Bobby the lovely, portly old gentleman

female puppy died within about an hour of arriving here but the male puppy survived and I decided to keep him. I called this one Bobby and he had such character but he was pretty full-on. He was an arrogant little chap and Flash, one of our German Shepherds, would only put up with a certain amount of behaviour from Bobby. When Flash had had enough, he would press down with his huge paws on Bobby's head and not stop until Bobby clearly calmed down and stopped whatever was irritating Flash.

Bobby could irritate me in the car since he would bark continuously. If he saw a bicycle, he would bark; if he saw pram, he would bark; and it drove me mad. He barked nearly all the way to Glasgow on one particular journey. So, I purchased a citronella collar and only had to inflict the spray on him once. After that, I did not even need to put the collar part on him: all I had to do was let him see me about to press the button. If I caught sight of a bicycle

I would say 'Bobby!' and let him see me holding the button which was enough to stop him barking, although he would be shaking with excitement at the sight of the bike. Bobby died when he was only eight years old from cancer.

I have seen a lot more cases of cancer and skin problems amongst dogs nowadays. I wonder whether this has something to do with the processed foods they are fed or our obsession with hygiene and over-use of cleaning products. We wash their bedding in detergent, and shampoo the carpets they lay on and use so many sprays and polishes in our homes that they are breathing in all these chemicals. They are usually physically closer to them so cannot escape their fumes.

Graham has started work on the isolation block. This is a quieter area that we use for dogs that are poorly or recovering from an operation. It is a good spot for a bitch and her litter of puppies or if a dog is very distressed by the main kennel environment and needs a bit of time to settle down. The three enclosures within the block are much easier to clean since they are now lined with the sort of material you would use to line a wet-room. The smallest of the three enclosures has underfloor heating, so seriously ill animals can have a bit of extra comfort. Harling will make the outside look better and once hatch doors are installed in each pen the dogs will be able to enjoy some outside space. At the moment, they depend upon someone having to put them on a lead and take them out to it but at least the pens are large.

They say, 'make hay while the sun shines' and so harling was put on hold on the first good day this week when Graham and our old tractor took the opportunity to mow the grass for hay. We have, potentially, around £7,000 worth of hay and we need at least £4,000 of that for our own use here. We can sell the rest and use some of that money to pay for the fertiliser, which cost £1,000 this year. The cut grass had been turned for the third time but then it started to rain again. If we do lose the whole lot it will have to go to someone for silage and we will have to buy in hay.

Everything is going well in readiness for the annual fete. The minibus to carry people and dogs from the field car park is booked; Colin, the chap who cooks the burgers, sausages and bacon has confirmed he will be here; the stallholders have confirmed; and the prizes are sorted. We are waiting for the rosettes to come and I still need to find the time to prepare the forms for the dog show, but I've got a few weeks yet. I have to do what I can, when I can, because there is so much to do and the phone never stops. I counted thity-two calls between 9am and 4.30pm on one day this week, and that was by no means out of the ordinary.

People complain that I have not answered their phone call but I can only respond to one call at a time. If we could afford to have someone, like a receptionist, answering telephone calls they could probably provide responses to maybe forty per cent of the calls, such as those that require a specific answer to a specific question. There are other phone calls that require an immediate decision that has to come from me, so a receptionist would have to locate me rather than tell the caller they will ring them back and these kinds of calls could go back and forth endlessly. The kind of calls I alone can respond to are things like the call this week from a lady who had a tiny kitten that had been trodden on by accident and they did not have the money for the vet; I had to make an immediate decision since it appeared to have broken its neck. I do understand what it is like to have absolutely no money, since this was my situation at one point, so I know how I would have felt if an emergency had occurred and I was desperate.

Week 6

The hay is now baled, much to our relief since we thought we had lost the lot due to the weather. When we checked the hay last Saturday it was sodden in all our fields and, when you picked it up and looked underneath, what should have been green hay looked as if it was black. As soon as the weather improved a bit, Graham and Hamish, a kind neighbour, turned it again a couple of times and with a bit more sunshine Graham was able to bale it. Now he is busy trying to get 1,900 bales, the best crop we have ever had, into the sheds. Of course, erecting the second-hand barn we bought has been put on hold, as has work on the isolation block, since the hay has taken priority.

There are a lot of smaller animals such as guinea pigs and rabbits coming in at the moment. This is always the case in the first couple of weeks of the summer school holidays. It is a bit like the influx of older dogs coming in before Christmas and the puppies coming in during early spring when they have stopped being cute and become a nuisance. Do I sound cynical?

The St Bernard, whose owner had been taken into hospital, has arrived so we now have twenty-five dogs in the kennels. Some of the dogs are doubling up in a kennel, especially those that came in together from the same home and that relieves a bit of pressure on space. Fortunately, a couple of dogs who came in last week have gone out to new homes because they were just lovely good-natured creatures and quickly took someone's fancy.

Another kennel has been vacated by Betty, the German Shepherd bitch that was handed over last week because her owner had problems managing her. He changed his mind this week and she has gone back to him after we had a long talk. I offered advice about her management, including a suggestion that she is spayed

Go on: give us a home, purrrrr-please

and that he and his dog come up to MAA every day to walk with an experienced dog walker. The aim is to get her used to being around people and dogs and to improve her walking on a lead. He has done this every day since then and we hope the problems will lessen: she is a dog with so much potential and he clearly cares for her. She was thrilled to see him.

The police have brought in a big dog that clearly is not well and needs to go to the vet urgently. It transpires that it has a heart problem, a skin problem, sore joints, a urinary infection, bad teeth and its ears are in a terrible state. We got everything we could get done at the first visit, just to make the dog more comfortable, but it is booked in again next week to get its teeth and ears sorted under anaesthetic. However, the vets want to run blood tests. This too is a dog whose owner has been taken into hospital, so I have to get the owner's permission for these tests. Trying to find out the owner's name and whereabouts from the police has been a nightmare. The Data Protection Act, whilst intended to protect everyone's privacy, is also a source of great problems. When common sense tells you what should be done, you find the Act prevents this. It took me so long to get enough information to enable me to contact the owner and obtain her permission. When a similar situation occurs in the future I am going to refuse to take the dog unless the police or social services get permission to give me the information I need to care for the animal properly.

The dog is looking a lot more comfortable now, especially since we gave it a lovely bath, shampooing right down to the skin but my worry is whether all this will be continued when it returns to its owner. Is the owner going to be fit enough to care for it and to get appropriate veterinary care for it since these are ongoing health problems?

It makes me very sad when I have to hand back an animal that I know needs a lot of care that they are unlikely to get, judging by the condition in which they came in. We can do so much for an animal whilst it is here but when I have to hand it back to an uncertain future, it makes me sick. In my heart, I know that in a month's time that animal will be back in the same awful condition it was in when it came in to MAA, but there is nothing I can do about it as the law stands. Sometimes, I do ask the SSPCA to keep an eye on an animal but I tell the owner I have done this and the reason.

An elderly German Shepherd Dog, Clyde, went out to a home but, unfortunately, he is back. It did not work out because he did not get on with one of their other dogs, so he is back but he seems to have resettled straight away, as if he has just come back home. He likes his walks and the walkers like him. He enjoys his food and watching all the comings and goings in the kennel block. And, he definitely enjoys treats but he rarely rests completely.

Scruffy, a very attractive, rough-coated, black dog with a cheeky face, took the fancy of a couple who called in this week. They came back to have another look at him and decided he was the dog for them. He is very excitable in a nervy way but they did not mind. He came to us with no social skills at all and had never been on a lead. It took a lot of effort trying to get him to walk on a lead and one of the dog walkers spent a lot of time with Scruffy trying to help him develop a few manners. Fingers crossed that the relationship with his new owners blossoms.

We received a wee Jack Russell via the Dog Warden and its owners collected it next day. However, we heard on the grape vine that it was back wandering on and off which is concerning for safety

Tara – butter would not melt in her mouth!

reasons because it is an accident waiting to happen. Just as concerning is the fact that we have now heard she is in season! Any male dog, from a Jack Russell to a Great Dane, will try to mate with her and this is potentially very dangerous for the wee dog. My own view is that if a dog is straying on a number of occasions, then the Dog Warden should be able to collect the dog and it not be returned to its owners since they are unable to prevent it getting out. However, as the law stands, the Dog Warden can keep collecting the dog, bringing it here, and the owners collecting it time and time again.

In my garden, I have a cotoneaster that has been there since my childhood. It is in flower at the moment and is alive with bees. The buzzing is really loud, as if the bush itself is humming and wonderful to stand and listen to. However, Tara, our GSD puppy, is also showing an interest in it and I watched her sitting still for a full minute, listening to the bees. She spends all her waking hours wondering what she can get up to next, so she is in for a nasty surprise if she makes a grab for the bees! This week, when I was unloading the shopping, I put two one-litre bottles of fizzy drink down by the door but when I returned from putting stuff in the fridge, there was only one. There was Tara running around carrying the full bottle. My fear was that she would puncture it and it would explode but she put it down when I yelled. She loves taking things and Graham found a big heavy wrench by the gate but we have no idea where she picked it up from.

One of our own rescued Border Collies, Moss, has been with us for four years and to this day had never walked on a lead. Moss was a poor nervous dog when he came into the kennels. He was frightened of the noise, the dogs and people and none of us could get him on a lead. I wanted so much to get Moss up to our house, but I never said that to Graham. I thought that if I could get Moss into a kennel up by the house he would do better away from the stress of the kennel block and he would calm down. However, I just knew Graham was not going to fall for it.

One day, I casually said to Graham that it would really be good if we could buy the kennel, along with its own run, that they were selling from Fettes Sawmill and, to my amazement, he said what a good idea it was. Within about two hours of us talking about the kennel, Graham had it here, all set up and I had Moss established in it. So, Graham had fallen for it!! Moss was only there for a couple of days before we let him out to join our own happy bunch of dogs and it was an instant success. Moss adored one of our dogs, called Ben, and followed him everywhere like a shadow.

Against Graham's advice, I decided to take Moss with the rest of our dogs for a walk in the wood beside the house. It was just too soon and he took off on his own and my sister telephoned to say Moss had just run through her garden and was heading off down the road. When we caught up with him, he was rounding up a neighbour's sheep. Graham managed to persuade him to follow him back into the wood and down to the house. He did make a break for it once more but came back on his own accord and has never done anything like that again. Whilst Moss accepted wearing a collar, we tried time and time again to put a lead on him, trying clip leads and loop leads, but he would freeze and turn into a shaking wreck he was so upset. This meant that while he could run around the yard here and go for his walk with us in the adjacent

Moss on a lead with Scampy and Tara

wood, he could not go out with us on one of the longer walks or to the seaside.

That is, until last Sunday. Graham just popped a clip lead on Moss's collar and there was no panic, so I took the lead from Graham and just walked. Four years we have tried but he obviously felt he was ready for it now. Unfortunately, we have been so occupied with wild animal feeding and preparing the place for our fete that we have not had the opportunity to take Moss for a lovely long walk on his lead, but we will.

Our other Border Collie, Scampy, came to us when he was about four weeks old having been found in a ditch, so he is used to a collar and lead. When he came to us, we sat him on the table next to a half-llitre milk carton and it was bigger than he was. Graham just picked the puppy up and slipped it inside his shirt, so, that was it, I knew from that moment that Scampy would never be rehomed to anyone except Graham.

We are caring for a feral mother cat, that I have named Minty, and her kittens. They were found under the stage at a popular rock concert venue. I am forcing my attention on the kittens so that they get used to people. One of them in particular will hiss loudly at me, and I hiss loudly back at it. Then it hisses again, but a bit more softly, and I hiss back more softly and so we carry on until it is just whispered hisses and, finally, it just stares at me. They are only

Steve the Stoat

about five weeks old now and at that age you can tame them down and gradually turn them into domestic cats. One in particular is already more interested in his food than in hissing and spitting, so he is up for it! All the kittens will definitely get homes but although mum is a young cat, hardly more than a kitten herself, I am not so sure about her. If she does not tame down then she will be neutered and stay here with all the other feral cats, but it would be nice to think Minty might end up in a loving domestic environment.

Torrential rain managed to destroy a number of nests resulting in baby birds being brought in and a wee hedgehog I have called Hoggy. He is almost spineless and sits comfortably in the palm of my hand. He is eating more like a horse than the tiny wee creature it is and, of course, Hoggy and all the baby birds need frequent feeding. One is a tiny baby dove and Graham has named it Eddie the Eagle.

I was reminded of Steve Stoat who was only 7cm long when he was brought to us. The person who found him had seen the mother stoat crossing the road carrying her babies but she had dropped this one and not returned to pick him up. We hand reared him which required a lot of care since with such a tiny creature it is all too easy to drown it when feeding and it needed to be kept at just the right temperature. We gradually reduced the amount of human contact and changed his food to more like the diet he would take in the wild. After five months Steve was very sturdy and was getting a wee bit cheeky and nippy, so he was definitely telling us he was ready to go back into his natural environment. When the press came to take a photograph of him just before he was released, he ran up the inside of Graham's trouser leg, much to his consternation and the amusement of the photographer.

Week 7

Poor old Bobby did not get his hoped for home since the couple who wanted to take him never returned. They were very keen on this lovely old chap but I have a feeling that the mention of a home check deterred them. Especially with a dog like Bobby, who loves people, loves walking, treats and a fuss but is not so keen on other dogs or animals, it is essential that we do a home visit because we know what kind of fencing and security arrangements need to be in place before he arrives. He is an older dog so he cannot go somewhere where he will constantly have to climb many stairs. We do not do home visits out of nosiness – we do them to increase the chances of dog and new owner having a good relationship but some folk find this intrusive or even insulting. Poor Bobby must wait again but Hunter, our 'barking chorus leader' went out to a home but only for the night since they said he never shut up!

Whenever there is a lot of barking in the night, Graham or I go to see what is happening. If nothing untoward is going on we usually yell, 'Shut-up the lot of you!' or words to that effect, and it goes absolutely silent. They look at us with a look of 'What?!' and then get quite waggy since they wonder if it might just be early breakfast time. Our very tolerant neighbours never complain about the noise and, hopefully, someone will come along who is able to provide this barking ring-leader with the time and activity level that he needs.

A wee Chihuahua who was signed over following a really dreadfully sad family bereavement was out for a walk on the beach with a couple of volunteers when he was spotted by a lady. It was love at first sight and, sensibly, the lady came into the kennels along with her Spaniel in order to walk the Chihuahua a couple of times, just to make sure the arrangement would work. And it has! The wee fellow has his forever home and our two volunteers have been back to the beach to see how things are going and it is a very happy relationship.

Another dog signed over to us came in because he had become destructive around the home. It is a big, youngish dog and it transpires that it has only been getting one short walk each day, as well as being left alone for quite long periods of time. Most dogs need a good amount of exercise, especially big dogs and all dogs need stimulation. When an adult dog is bored it will find something to do. An adult dog that is chewing is, usually, a dog that is bored. This particular dog is a Collie/Labrador and that breed especially needs stimulation, company and plenty of exercise. I am amazed by the number of people who do not realise how important it is to walk a dog and give it exercise. Of course, you use your sense and if, for example, it is very warm and you have an old dog with a heavy dark coat, then you wait for a part of the day when it is cooler. I honestly do not believe a dog is right for a household where everyone is out all day. Fortunately, this particular dog has gone out to a home where he should be able to get everything he needs.

Sometimes it becomes very busy in the kennel block and there can be a few folk waiting to be attended to. Most people understand the peaks and troughs that naturally occur and wait patiently until someone is free to attend to them. However, occasionally folk act as if they are the most important person and can be quite rude. This week, one such woman brought in a stray, for which we are most grateful. However, because there was only one person on duty in the kennel, and she was dealing with another stray that had come in, the woman became impatient and very rude. All she had been asked to do was to hang on with the dog until it could be properly checked in. We need to know, for instance, exactly where it was found, what time it was picked up, how it has behaved and we immediately check for microchip. We need to see the interaction between the person and the dog they have found since, sometimes, the so-called 'finder' is actually the dog's owner and they pretend it is a stray because they do not want to have to explain why they want to hand over their dog. We will never judge them since they could have just abandoned their pet, so we will do everything to make the handover as painless as possible. The woman ranted about not wanting to hang around, not having time to waste on things like this and then left the dog, backing out of the car park so quickly that she reversed into our wall, damaging her car – now, is that 'karma' or what!!

A local vet asked us to take a cat that had been brought in with a serious injury necessitating amputation of its tail and one hind leg. Fortunately, someone had found this poor cat in their garden and taken it to the vet. We confirmed we would take the cat and cover the vet's expenses. When it arrived with us it was eating and drinking fine but had a problem using the litter tray until we changed it for a seed tray with a lower edge and instead of cat litter we used compost. Unfortunately, his tail did not seem to be healing properly and he had to go back to the vet for a further operation. However, there was not much more tail they could take off because of something to do with the nerves in that area. The skin was not healing and last weekend he had to spend a couple of days on a drip but will be coming back to us at the end of the week, along with a very hefty bill! Arthur, as we have called him, will be able to go to a new home but it will not be easy to find someone who will want to care for this three-legged character.

To add to our ever-increasing cat population, a family handed in a twelve-year-old cat that they have had since it was a kitten. Apparently, their daughter was no longer interested in the cat and so they wanted it to go to another home. The poor cat was clearly stressed, not understanding why he was not back in the only home he had ever known. We managed to find someone who was willing to foster this cat but, although she tried, she was concerned that she was not going to be able to stop this very active cat from getting out and so he came back here until we could find him a more secure home. Much to our relief he was given a home. However, he was only out for a day and in torrential rain we were called to Dingwall to collect him. He had meowed all night and they could not stand it, so he is back in the cattery. At twelve he is still a very active cat, which was the reason the person who had tried the previous week to foster him had reluctantly returned him. He is also a very vocal cat so it is going to be a very special owner who rehomes and keeps this very loving elderly creature. You cannot be certain how long a cat will live: some go on into their twenties whilst others do not make it much beyond twelve. Although it is not easy to rehome an elderly dog, it is easier than getting someone to take on an older cat.

Still in torrential rain, Graham and I drove at high speed down to Aviemore to collect a kitten that, apparently, had a broken leg. We were told that the owners had no money, no transport and no way of getting the animal to a vet. The reason for our speed was because we had made an appointment with a local, regularly used veterinary practice and they wanted the kitten in by lunchtime to deal with its fractured leg. Not only did we subsequently realise that there was a veterinary practice within very easy walking distance from the kitten's home but when the vet examined the leg it was not broken, just badly bruised. I would have preferred to have the kitten signed over to MAA since it had never been inoculated, wormed, nor treated for fleas. However, the law requires me to return an animal to its owner if they want it back and, in this instance, it was a relative of the owners who collected this wee bundle of fur so, fingers crossed, I hope it now gets the care it needs. We wait to see if Graham gets a speeding ticket!

One of our many feral cats, called Archie, an older one, was unwell and was probably going into renal failure. We know these cats so well because only Graham and I deal with them on a daily basis and they know us, so they are calm around us. They have a nice natural environment where they can stay indoors in the warm, sleep in clean bedding, go out into their large enclosure, climb trees and prowl around, but you cannot sit and cuddle them because it would put them under so much stress. We, like a shepherd, know all of them and can spot when something is wrong or one is hiding itself. We check every day, for every cat, just as a shepherd would do with his flock and we can spot problems. We have to know when to draw the line with them and, after consulting the vet, the decision was made to put Archie to sleep.

Midge and Tensing, two large, fat domestic cats, have been rehomed together. They came in when their owner fell ill and had to make a difficult decision about whether she would be fit to continue to offer them the care they deserved. They have a lovely new home which is a good situation for them and for their previous owner, whose mind was put at ease. Tensing is a huge cat and will

*Morag hoping for
a custard cream*

shortly need some dental work done but I do not like saddling a new owner with a large bill straight away, so I have said MAA will pay for the dental work.

We have forty-three sheep at present. Some have been here for fifteen years and they have come from all sorts of places. Some were cruelty cases; some were taken as pets until the owners discovered they could not keep them; and some were orphaned lambs that we were asked to rear. We are very lucky that we have a shepherd in the family and so he has just been and sheared them. They are so much more comfortable now they do not have all that heavy wool on them. He is amazing at shearing them and never nicks their skin. The fleeces are, unfortunately, hardly worth anything nowadays compared to many years ago. Graham and I can trim their feet, no mean task since many of them are rather fat! They also have hard heads and I have the bruises to prove it!

I love having sheep around and we are a registered croft, so there are all sorts of regulations to comply with. Some of these sheep are real characters. Morag and Daisy were hand-reared on the bottle and were so poorly at first. They are now big healthy sheep and, although all our animals have the proper food for their breed as their main diet, they all get occasional treats. These two have a preference for custard creams and ginger nuts as a treat, although they are very 'brand aware' and will not accept cheaper brands! They now share their field with four goats, numerous chickens and Glen the goose who is in charge of all of them. Glen had a definite attitude problem when he was younger but age seems to have mellowed him a little. He has bitten me, bruising the

Charlie Drake

skin even through boots and jeans, and if the goats or sheep try to challenge him, he puts his neck out and the look on his face says, 'You really want to try me?' They invariably back off!

A friend of mine took Charlie Drake, a young duck handed in to us with a badly damaged wing, to join his other birds on the wonderful pond he dug by hand. Charlie Drake will never fly because of the damage and this friend's garden is fully fenced, so he would be safe. However, things do not always work to plan and it turned out that Charlie was terrified of the other ducks. Poor Charlie looked really stressed so we have him back here and put him in a private pen. His 'pond' is a big dog bed full of water, so he can stay there for a wee while. We will probably get his wing feathers taken off because they stick out at a very strange angle and it would be easier for him without them. He is never going to fly, so it makes no difference from that perspective. We have set up his pen right next to one of our cockerels and his five hens. That cockerel is an absolute darling: he is so good to his hens and when we got the two tiny white hens he used to sit with them under his wings at night and they still cuddle up to him each night. He never attacks anything and my hope is that the duck will eventually be able to join this chicken family. Our birds are shut in at night for safety, so flightless Charlie Drake will be safe. It is many years since we lost any animal, even though there are foxes about the area.

Two of our chickens were missing one night when we went to shut them in. We have wee houses dotted around for them but this pair was nowhere to be seen. My concern was that they were under a bush somewhere sitting on eggs and we really do not want to breed more chickens and definitely not another cockerel, so we had to find those eggs. They turned up as usual the next day, much to our relief, and were clearly not brooding eggs, but where had they been?

Our lovely boisterous puppy, Tara, managed to smash a very heavy dog bowl this week. This is a really heavy bowl that she picked up and, having hurled the water out all over the kitchen floor, she ran off with the bowl, dropping it in the yard where it smashed into many pieces. She has a 'thing' about water in bowls and, when she drinks, she swishes her head from side to side just to see the water flying all over the place. Graham found an even bigger and heavier water bowl with a shallower lip which would make it more difficult for her to get her jaw around and pick up. 'She will never be able to pick that up,' he said. Wrong – it was more difficult to pick it up but she managed to half carry and half drag it from the kitchen, through the hall and out, spilling all the water in the process. At least we got it back before she broke it. Her latest antic was to roll a black plastic dustbin around the yard, much to her enjoyment. Tara is such a happy puppy and you can see her thinking what she can do next when our other dogs do not want to play with her.

Hoggy the hedgehog gave me fright this week. We use a lot of puppy pads for various reasons at MAA and one use is to line Hoggy's box. When I went to his box to give him his first feed of the day, Hoggy was nowhere to be seen. He was not under the puppy pad and I felt a rush of panic until I saw a small lump and

Eddie the Eagle

realised that he had split the layers of the pad and put himself in between them. He is still too little to roll himself up, and, of course, he is so used to being handled that he does not roll defensively, and his spines are only just starting to toughen up. Although he is still far too tiny to be released, when he is ready to go I have a home for him with someone who has a secure walled garden and can keep an eye on him. Even though Hoggy has been hand-reared there will be a point when nature kicks in and he will adopt the same behaviour as a wild hedgehog. Any wild animal that I take in, I do it with the intention of a release back into the wild, except the feral cats.

Eddie the Eagle has nearly doubled in size and is getting feathered and, please God, in a week or so he will start eating for himself, since he has an amazing appetite for one so small. I have discovered a great way of feeding baby birds: I use a teat off a feeding bottle and put the food inside it so that their beak goes in, mimicking the way the mother feeds them. I am forever trying to clean the baby bird, since he manages to get the food all over his face and neck while he eats. I have started scattering some seed around in the hope he will start to pick it up and then they quickly lose interest in the teat. It is going to break my heart when this wee bird has to go but once he is able to fly he has to go because we have too many cats here. I did have a hand-reared pigeon called Percy Pigeon for his entire life. Percy was free to come and go but chose to stay and he would follow me and the dogs around the wood on our walks, diving down over the dog's heads. Percy survived but I just feel there are too many cats wandering around here now to be sure Eddie the Eagle will be safe. I have a home lined up for him with someone who feeds a lot of birds within a safe garden area and although they have taken a cat from MAA, it does not bother with birds.

We had a lovely family come into MAA to say thank you, in person, for the financial help we gave them when an unexpected veterinary bill arrived. This coincided with a job loss and a new job that did not pay anything for the first month. As well as saying 'thank-you' they put what they could in one of our collecting boxes. Sometimes, we get a card to say 'thank-you' and sometimes someone will pay the money back bit by bit over a period of time, and this is so much appreciated. We are not all about the money but the least folk can do is to give us a quick phone call or a wee note to let us know how the animal is progressing but maybe they think we are not interested, so they do not bother. I jokingly say that maybe one of the people whose pet we have helped will win the lottery and remember this charity!

Week 8

July has just started to look a bit like summer, which cheers everyone up. The daily round of feeding, cleaning, feeding and cleaning continues for our wild animals and Minty and her kittens. As they all improve and grow they demand more food, demanding it loudly. Eddie the Eagle, our baby dove, is looking like a miniature dove now, with feathers and the right body shape but he is constantly in need of cleaning since his eating habits get worse not better! He now sits on my arm, or on my head, whilst demanding food. Whenever he sees or hears me, even if it is 11pm when we have finished walking our own dogs, he squawks as loudly as he can to remind me that he would like his supper.

Minty is in disgrace since she has vandalised the vinyl flooring in the hallway, and I mean vandalised it. Initially, I had them in a guinea pig run because if you can confine a feral cat and its kittens you can tame them down. However, she vandalised the guinea pig run and broke out so we decided she would be safe in the bottom part of the guinea pig run but loose in our hallway area. This gave her more space and she could entertain herself by looking out of the windows. By the time we noticed what she was doing she had shredded the vinyl into hundreds of tiny pieces and so we have decided to relocate her and her kittens to new quarters in a big rabbit run. So, they are outside in a safe, padlocked setting and with a cosy place to curl up in. We can still handle the kittens and mum seems to be a bit better behaved. Perhaps what she wanted was to be outside. We can do nothing but go and buy new vinyl, which does not come cheap even though the new stuff is as thin as paper! The good news is that the people up at the concert venue where cat and kittens came from would like to have mum back, neutered of course, so no more kittens. She will be ready for neutering in a couple of weeks and the kittens will be about eight weeks old then, so they can go to new homes.

On 20th July, I was invited to judge the dog show at the Sutherland Agricultural Show. Sutherland is the biggest county in the United Kingdom, stretching from the Atlantic to the North Sea. I have been invited to judge a few shows now and I never know what to expect. I know that I am dealing with people all day, every day at MAA but I am not really the most outgoing person and I am quite nervous about these shows. It still is not my favourite pastime but I am getting better. Graham came along with me this time and was really happy because there was a lot of machinery and vintage tractors, so he was in his element while I judged fourteen classes. The classes include such things as best puppy and best veteran dog but there are also more unusual classes such as the waggiest tail and the best six legs! As you would expect, every one of those dogs was in beautiful condition: very cared for dogs and very proud owners. No matter who was awarded first, everybody clapped and cheered and it was just good fun since people were not taking it too seriously.

There was one class that was quite difficult and that was the one for best rescue dog. There were nine dogs in this class and a couple were ex-MAA dogs. One was a beautiful Lurcher who had put his owners through a few hoops before he finally settled down. In the ring, this lovely dog played shamelessly to the crowd, rolling upside down and shuffling along on his tummy to chat to other dogs – clearly, a star. However, the dog that won deserved the prize because he had experienced a dreadful life before he came to Munlochy, evidenced by the number of scars and old injuries he carried. However, someone took this pathetic wreck of a dog home with them and he had made such progress. It was looking fit and healthy, thanks to the hard work of its owners. So this dog was awarded first prize and its owners were absolutely over the moon. I have judged a show where I was supposed to judge the best pet and how on earth do you judge between rabbits, budgies, cats and dogs – you do your best.

This week, there have been a lot of folk visiting the kennel block to look at the dogs with the possibility of rehoming them. Some dogs go amazingly quickly and one that was signed over in the morning was spotted by a family known to MAA and after taking it for a walk, and getting lots of cuddles, it went out in the same evening.

One of our long-stay Lurchers that, along with his partner, had a failed rehoming a few weeks ago has been given a second chance. Initially, I wanted this pair to go together but this one was easier to rehome and I did not want to spoil his chances. The people who have taken him this time have had dogs from us before and family connections in this area, although they live in the central belt. Our Lurcher is going to be renamed immediately since his original name does not suit him: he will be Monty from now on. I am touching wood because he is a nice dog and deserves a home after all this time. Now we need a home for his partner who is not quite such an easy-going character.

Monty's new owners have not telephoned to say there are any problems, so, hopefully, no news is good news. I have not telephoned them, though I will do next week. I try not to telephone folk too soon after a rehoming since a lot of people tell me that during that first week there were many times when they thought the dog would have to come back. In those first few days with a new animal in the house, you are learning about that animal and it is learning about you and what is expected of it. In those early days, many people say, 'What have we done!', and then the bond starts to develop and after ten days to a fortnight, they start to enjoy each other's company. Quite soon they say, 'We wouldn't be without it!' and 'It's the best thing we have ever done!'

I always tell people I will take a dog back straight away in that first month and that it must come back to MAA and not be passed on to anyone else. I do not get them to sign an agreement to this effect since it has been proved by other charities that it just does not work: people will sign anything and then just ignore it. As far as I know, there have only been one or two situations in the past year where someone has passed a dog on to someone else and it is really disappointing, since I did not expect this. As it happens, it has probably worked out fine, but I will never let them have another dog from MAA since I cannot trust them.

The other lucky dog that got a home nearly did not because it 'did a runner'! One of our dog walkers took this lovely Collie walking and she managed to slip her lead and escape in the forest. Quickly alerted to this, two of our other walkers got their own dog out of the car and took it into the forest knowing that a dog will often join another dog, and it worked. This was fortunate because the dog in question got herself chosen by a lovely couple later that day and went to a new home the next day.

This incident reminded me of another occasion some time ago when one of our experienced dog walkers took a dog into the wood some distance from the kennels. The dog got off its lead and bolted with the dog walker in pursuit. The dog just hared straight home to the kennels and we waited for the dog walker to also come haring round the same corner, red-faced, sweating and gasping for breath. I had better not tell you what he called the dog when he got his breath back enough to speak. Even dogs that walk sedately on the outward trip often speed up on the return trip towards the kennels, which may be something to do with the fact that they know their grub will be ready!

Most MAA dogs are rehomed to folk in the Highlands but they have even gone as far as Hampshire on the south coast of England to friends of a friend. These people, who own an estate in Hampshire, were up on holiday visiting a friend of ours and came in, just to look around. They fell for a mother Lurcher and her puppy and the likelihood is that they will be up on holiday again this year and will bring the dogs to visit us.

We have had a number of strays brought in this week including a lovely-natured Staffie who came in with the police at 10.30pm and was collected later that same night by very concerned owners who did not care what time of night it was. Graham and I would rather have liked to go to our bed and let them collect the dog in the morning!

The elderly St Bernard who stayed with us while her owner was in hospital was not a well dog, as the vet confirmed. Whilst it was with us its condition was closely monitored and after the vet took blood samples, with the owner's permission, his advice was that the kindest thing to do was to put the animal to sleep. Fortunately, the owner was not in hospital very long and wanted to be there when her dog was euthanised, which was arranged. A sad end but

Those lovely eyes

it is something we all have to face when it is the best thing for the animal.

I really hate having to discuss euthanasia with owners, especially when it is in response to an animal's aggression. We had a telephone call from a chap who said the SSPCA had suggested he telephone MAA for advice. His dog had started to attack him and his partner and they were being seriously bitten. The attacks were getting worse and he wondered if we would be prepared to take his dog. After getting a lot more information about what had been going on and was going on at the moment, I raised the subject of euthanasia, since it sounded like there was something very wrong with this dog. He said this had been discussed but when they found out how much it would cost they could not afford it.

I could tell by the way the conversation had gone that these people really cared about the animal and the chap was finding it quite hard to talk at that point. I pointed out that the dog might attack someone other than him and his wife and that could have really dreadful consequences including legal action. He agreed, saying he could understand what I was saying. I asked how much he could afford and I suggested that if he took it to the vet, explained the situation and that MAA had agreed to foot the part of the bill he could not pay, he could save himself and the dog getting into a worse situation. He was relieved and did it before another attack took place.

The very next day we got a phone call just after 7am from some-one who had taken a Jack Russell from us the previous day. We had explained that this dog had bitten in the past and this was why he had been brought to MAA. The previous owners told us that his aggressive behaviour became worse as the day progressed and he was at his worst after dark. However, he had been behaving himself during the weeks he was in the kennel, going for walks with various dog walkers, getting petted and so on and nobody had been bitten. He had shown no inclination to bite even when we were doing the evening rounds, feeding him, letting him out to spend a penny and settling him for bed. Unfortunately, he had bitten his new owner that first night and it was a nasty bite, so we drove over to collect him once we had finished the morning feeding round.

What we saw was a really serious bite that had followed an unprovoked attack. We talked about it and decided that, in view of the nature of this bite, which was serious enough to necessitate a hospital visit, we would be taking him on a one-way trip to the vets. The lady who had been bitten felt awful about this outcome, saying she had wanted to give the wee chap a chance but recognised she could not put up with this. You cannot live with a dog you cannot trust, especially if you become afraid of it. It is never something we feel good about but the reputation of MAA is at stake. Folk trust us to be honest with them and ensure, to the best of our ability, their safety. Something was just not right with this dog and I was not going to take the risk of giving him another chance and it ending up in something even more serious.

Last year, we only had to have one dog put down due to aggression but this year we have had three already. We cannot keep taking in and passing on dogs that are potentially dangerous. It does nobody, and especially not the dog, any good to keep going out and coming back. We give them months in the kennels if necessary during which time we monitor their behaviour and try to find out if something scares the dog or provokes it. So long as we can see something in the dog that makes us think they can learn and can change we will continue their rehabilitation. In the kennel, we are continually socialising a dog: it is as if it is on the 'naughty step' and we are controlling what it does. It is fed at the same time, exercised at the same time by different people, and there are always people coming and going and stopping to talk to it. This socialisation process can work for some dogs but sometimes it is too dangerous to try. Sometimes it appears that there is something really wrong with the dog mentally. It is the part of the job that I hate.

When we had a pack of six German Shepherd Dogs brought in by the police, taken from the same owner who was arrested and prosecuted, they were all extremely reactive and one in particular was more so than the others. However, there was something in them that gave us hope and although it took a long time, they were all rehabilitated and successfully rehomed into forever homes. They were lovely dogs once out of the horrendous situation in which they had existed but it was a slow process. In the beginning, they would hurl themselves at the kennel doors, snarling and barking and really meaning business. Our dog walkers were told not to stand looking at these dogs but to stand as close as safely possible with their backs turned on the dogs and then just walk away. We gave them no attention when they were behaving outrageously and it kind of confused them because nobody was reacting aggressively in return to their aggression. It is similar to how you might treat a really naughty toddler having a tantrum. Initially, I was the only one who walked these big, potentially dangerous GSDs. Hour upon hour I walked them, since they were all big dogs who needed plenty of exercise. Then Graham began walking them and then other experienced dog walkers took them walking. There is a lovely picture of all six of these dogs standing together with me when their new owners brought them back for a visit to our annual fete. All six of them have since passed away but at least they enjoyed a number of years.

We have now purchased special locks for the windows in some of the rooms in our house because we sometimes have cats staying with us while their owners are away and there is no other space available. We will be looking after four cats for people who are moving up from the south and if they are anything like our own cats, they will know how to rattle and manipulate window handles, hence the new locks.

The five most recent feral cat acquisitions are taming down nicely. We are still keeping them in their private quarters in the hope

Playing peek-a-boo

they will become tame enough to rehome in a domestic situation. If they have to go into the main feral cat houses then they will but I would like to keep the numbers down as much as possible and these five continue to show possibilities. They are very clean cats, always using their litter tray which is a good sign and they are responding more calmly around humans, albeit just Graham and me at present.

Week 9

Well, it's August and it feels like summer at last, although we are getting plenty of rain too. It was a really hot day when a young badger was found lying at the side of the road out Drumnadrochit way. He was unresponsive when the folk picked him up and they did not know whether he was ill or had been knocked by a car. When he arrived here I took him straight to the vet who could find nothing wrong with him, except that he was alive with a million fleas! The fleas were visible on the surface, which is a sure sign that he had been cold; otherwise the fleas would stay closer to his warm skin. He was washed down and a lot of the fleas were washed away, but it was done more to check if he had any wounds hidden beneath his fur that we could not easily see. He had no external wounds, so perhaps he had just become dehydrated during that very hot spell. He was not thin enough to suggest he had been starving or ill for some time and, although he was very subdued initially, he quickly recovered here, eating very well indeed. As soon as we could, we took him back to exactly where he was found and released him. We never keep a wild animal for longer than is absolutely necessary. We are also aware, from past experience, that badgers can be very aggressive once they are on the mend!

MAA is on a register of organisations offering experience for youngsters such as those working towards a Duke of Edinburgh Award and experience for disabled people who want to spend some time with animals. This week, we had a visit from a young girl who wanted to walk one of our dogs. She came with a carer and together they took one of our more gentle dogs for a walk. The look of total joy on the girl's face was wonderful and when they returned they asked if they could come back next week and the answer, of course, was 'certainly'. There is something very special about being around animals and working with dogs in particular. Some of our disabled visitors get a lot of pleasure from just looking at whatever we happen to have on site at that time, be it guinea pigs, rabbits, sheep or horses. Just stroking and cuddling an animal can lift your spirits and there is a lot of researched evidence that it can lower both blood pressure and pulse and release calming hormones. There is some evidence that it reduces perception of pain. Of course, walking dogs also provides exercise in the fresh air, so it is good for both mental and physical wellbeing.

Our visitors love to see animals such as hedgehogs that they may never have seen up close. Hoggy, our baby hedgehog, was very happy when he was introduced to another hedgehog that was handed in this week. The new hedgehog, who adores being stroked under his chin, is bigger than Hoggy – in fact, he is a bit of a pudding, so that is his name! The vet seemed to think there was nothing much wrong with Pudding, so it will be found a home as quickly as possible. I am not certain now whether the home I had in mind for the two of them to go to, with its walled garden, is as safe as I had thought. I have since heard that the area around there used to have loads of hedgehogs but, of late, there are hardly any. This makes me wonder what is happening to them: has some virus wiped them out or is there a shortage of food?

A pigeon was brought in after being mauled by a cat. After examining it, our vet thought it might be best to amputate its leg since it was at a most peculiar angle. Apparently, a bird can manage on one leg and it does not impede its flight. However, overnight its leg turned itself in the right direction and although the foot was still balled-up, it was managing to hop around quite happily. As soon as it got the chance, it was off like a rocket, so that was a very happy ending, and that is the kind we like.

The Dog Warden arrived with a Staffordshire Bull Terrier that had been tied up outside Eastgate Shopping Centre in Inverness. It had neither shade nor access to water on a really hot afternoon. The police were called by concerned members of the public, along with the Dog Warden, who brought the dog into MAA. The dog seemed all right but had an old infected cut on its leg that needed attention, so I made another trip to the vet, the third that day. The

Hoggy and Pudding

police, the Warden and I knew who the dog belonged to because we have been involved with it and its owner before. Two days later this woman's other dog was brought here by the police after it was found straying. When the owner was once again in a fit state to get here and retrieve her dogs, both of whom she adores, we had no choice but to hand them over, but it was with a heavy heart. We will see them again, for sure.

We had another two dogs brought in by the police this week when their owner was arrested. Once again, these dogs were well looked after and very much loved but we do not know how long we will be looking after them, depending upon what happens to their owner. Owners are usually grateful that their pet has been looked after during their absence and, if they can, they make a donation towards costs we have incurred, especially if we have had to spend out on veterinary fees whilst their pet has been with us.

Strays are a different matter. If we receive a stray from the Dog Warden, the owner is asked to pay the Highland Council a £25 uplift fee and all of that goes to the council. Most strays are reclaimed by their owners on the day they are brought in by the warden and I make no charge for caring for the animal, although a donation is always welcome. Sometimes, I will have had to take it to the vet immediately if it has some injury that it possibly sustained whilst straying and MAA foots the bill unless the owner offers to refund the money. If a stray is with us for more than one night, I can apply a kennelling fee of £14 per day to cover our costs. If a stray is not reclaimed for seven days then we can bill Highland Council for kennelling at 7x £14 per day. After that, all the costs are down to MAA.

Some days are more exhausting than others. On a scorching hot day this week, it was the day from hell. All the kennel staff were either off sick, on holiday or on a day off. My friend who would help out under these circumstances was not able to and Graham had to deal with all the other animals so I could deal with the kennel block. It was a day when we were open to the public and the fine weather seemed to bring out a lot of folk who were possibly looking to give one of our dogs a new home. It was a particularly hectic day, strays coming in with the Dog Warden and the police and dogs being signed over for rehoming by their owners. The kennel block was absolutely buzzing and the phone never stopped ringing.

The good thing was that one of the dogs signed over on that day, a lovely gentle Border Collie, went out straight away to a couple I know well and who have taken other dogs from us over the years. Another couple brought in a stray and had fallen for it just on the journey bringing it from where they found it to MAA. They asked if they could rehome it if its owner did not claim it within the seven day period. They would have been lovely owners but, unfortunately, the dog was reclaimed by an owner who was more annoyed that his dog had inconvenienced him than relieved that it was safe and sound. At 3.30pm I realised that I had not stopped all day and had not had anything to eat since breakfast at 8am, so I was very hungry. Of course, after something to eat, it all starts again when we do the evening feeding and exercise rounds. What a day!

I have already mentioned that we have converted one of our bedrooms into accommodation for cats since we had four cats booked in to stay with us whilst their owners relocated from the south. As it happened, only three of these four cats arrived, the fourth having 'done a runner' on the moving day, but a neighbour is caring for it until its owners can return south to collect it. The three who stayed with us have now gone to their new home and it gave us an opportunity to test out the possibility of using adapted bedrooms when we run out of space. With our newly installed window locks we can be sure feline guests stand no chance of 'doing a runner' from here!

Arthur, the three-legged and tailless cat, is still in residence here and still having cream applied to his tail wound each day. His lampshade protective collar was taken off because it was making him too hot but he is showing no signs of worrying his tail wound. I am going to see if one of the newspapers will run an article on him and see if that generates any interest from someone who will give him a home.

This week, I had to make the decision I hate to have to make. We have had a Border Collie here for some time now and we were told he had a history of 'nipping' when he was brought in. I always give dogs time to settle in, but this dog was a real worry. He did not settle and tried to bite a couple of people and this was definitely more than an attempt at 'nipping'. I can usually tell if we are going to be able to make progress with a dog, even the ones that seem highly reactive initially, but I was concerned that he was really dangerous. One of our regular dog walkers took a particular interest in this dog and walked him daily, trying to make a relationship with him. This particular walker is fervently against euthanasia for any animal unless on health grounds but he, along with all the other kennel staff and a couple of other regular volunteers, was in agreement that there was something about this dog that made them feel unsafe. Having talked to them all about the very unwelcome prospect of euthanasia, they were all in agreement that it needed to be done sooner rather than later, when someone might have been badly hurt. If any one of them had said they thought we should wait a while, then it would have been something we all needed to talk more about, but they all thought he was dangerous, so he was taken to be put to sleep. What made it so much worse was that, physically, he was a healthy dog who was not very old and I hated doing it, but we could not take the risk. Not a nice way to end the week.

Week 10

My mother in law got a nasty surprise this week. She was delivering some donated foodstuffs that she had collected for us, when lovely Cooper, our deaf Border Collie arrived back from a walk, just as excited as when he had left. He was on a long lead, and before the walker could stop him, Cooper jumped up and bit her on the bottom. The strength with which he grabbed at her was enough to make a puncture mark and her backside went every shade of blue, purple and green. She also, as a precaution, had a tetanus injection and Cooper is now walked on a short rather than long lead.

A more unusual visitor this week was a red kite who was suspected of having flown into some wire fencing. We took him straight off to the vet who checked him over and found bruising, especially around his neck, but no fractures anywhere. Once he recovered from the shock of it all he took some food and his neck straightened up, so he was going to make it. One of the officers from the Royal Society for the Protection of Birds came to see him. He checked which bird this was since he had been wearing a satellite tracking device which had got broken. A new satellite tracker was fitted before we released him a couple of days later, watched by BBC Alba. The RSPB officer was satisfied that there was no problem with the bird's take-off and he was flying fine. However, the bird decided to land in one of our trees in the yard and was still there in the evening. It was moving around and did not seem to be in any distress, so we put out food for the night and eventually he took off. It will be good to hear from the RSPB where this particular bird travels.

We enjoyed two more releases this week. We were able to release the young pigeon we have been nursing. He was flying well and able to use his injured leg to walk, even though the foot was still balled up. The baby seagull, who has been staying here to recover from an injury, was finally removed from his private enclosure and transferred to the bigger area to join the two seagulls who, because they will never be able to fly, are permanent residents here. Whilst they are locked into a shed at night, just for safety, their day enclosure is open and it meant that as soon as he could fly he could make his own decision on whether to stay or leave. He made that decision immediately and flew straight off. This was good news, firstly because he has healed and was ready to leave and, secondly, because he was always very vocal early in the morning, screaming loudly from his pen and setting off various other birds. However, he now returns, as soon as it is light, to perch just outside our bedroom window and scream loudly for food, just as he did in his enclosure.

Baby dove, aka Eddie the Eagle, is causing us grief! What was once a little featherless scrap is now a small, fit dove, feeding himself copious amounts of food and flying around our porch, safe from the cats. There is nothing wrong with his bowels, as our porch floor can testify. He still coos and shivers whenever he sees us, since this is how he asks to be fed and his favourite perch is on Graham or my head or shoulder. Despite the fact that we never keep a wild animal longer than is necessary, and I know this whenever I take on the task of hourly feeding, cleaning, and nurturing a tiny wild creature such as this chap, I worry about what will become of them once released. We have tried to distance ourselves from him in the build-up to a release but who could resist giving him a little stroke, which he clearly enjoys! We need to find him a safe haven but do not want him to go to an aviary. So, do we risk letting him loose around here and hope that, since the weather is getting colder, our cats will be more inclined to stay indoors?

This week, it was really hot on a couple of days, but we have had some awful weather with loud thunder, lightning flashes, and torrential rain. Fortunately, our own dogs take no notice of thunder and lightning, even though it started when we were out for a nice long walk. My telephone was constantly ringing with concerned owners whose dogs had fled in terror. A number of terrified dogs were brought in that day but reunited with their owners that night.

It amazes me that people, knowing their dog is worried by loud bangs, do not put it on a lead as soon as the sky darkens and the rumbles begin. Every time this weather descends upon us, we get people ringing up after their dog has jumped the garden fence or escaped in a panic. There is usually a warning of thunder and lightning, either on the weather forecast or just because the sky has gone black, so why not make sure the dog is called inside?

The council dog warden brought in a stray found on Rosemarkie beach. When I checked the microchip, it showed that it was owned by someone in Shropshire, so, clearly, the dog had not walked from there to Rosemarkie. Lots of dogs get brought into here when they are on holiday with their owners and, unfortunately, the owner has not provided the microchip company with a current mobile phone number so that the holidaying owner can be contacted. In this particular instance, the owners contacted us by chance and collected their dog very quickly. I expect some folk reading this book are now wondering whether they too have updated their details with the microchip companies! Imagine what it must be like to have to return without your beloved pet.

Readers may remember one of our long-stay Lurchers was rehomed and given a new name. Monty, as he became, has not been returned to the kennel by his new owners, although he has sorely tested their resolve. He has managed to run off a couple of times and has chewed up all manner of bits in their home. Fortunately, he sleeps all night in his bed outside their bedroom and is brimming full of energy the next day. He was always going to be hard work until he is 'tamed', socialised and settled into his new life since he and his partner in crime were virtually feral dogs, having had no training at all before they came to MAA. His new owners can still laugh about his antics, so I am hopeful he has found his forever home. Now, I just need to find someone who is experienced with lurchers and can cope with Speedy. Speedy is adorable but gets very over- excited when he meets other dogs and will snap in this situation so he is now being taken for walks wearing a muzzle which does not seem to bother him at all.

We are currently caring for two lovely dogs whilst one of their owners undergoes major surgery in Aberdeen and her husband goes over to visit. They come into MAA for a couple of days and

Speedy

then get collected to go back home until her husband goes back to Aberdeen. These two much-loved dogs really do not look happy in our kennels and the only time they cheer up is when someone takes them for a walk. They cannot wait to get back home for good and their owner can't wait to have them back.

Both Pudding, the big hedgehog, and Hoggy, the baby, are doing well and, for reasons of hygiene, have been moved out of my sitting room into a shed. Hedgehogs have quite an overwhelmingly strong and lingering smell, so I had to shampoo the carpet to try to freshen up the room they had been evicted from. They enjoy each other's company and neither of them rolls into a protective ball when I handle them. I have decided that neither of them will be going back to the wild until next spring, since Hoggy is still too small and, although Pudding could probably hibernate for two winters on his fat layer, Hoggy would miss his company.

I will, however, be looking for a home for Arthur, the three-legged, tailless cat who is now all healed up and getting around nicely. Little did I know when the vet rang me initially to ask if I would take on a cat that had been run over and needed a leg and tail amputation, that I would also get a bill for £1,500!

We are going to get another hefty bill in respect of a poor wee Westie who was signed over for rehoming this week. The poor creature has a dreadful skin problem: her chest, belly and legs being red raw and her eyes and ears in a pitiful state. I, along with many other people who saw her for the first time, felt physically sick and not a little angry that anyone could have allowed her to get into and remain in this painful and pitiful state. This did not happen overnight and she has suffered for a long time. Despite all of her troubles, Sophie is a gentle, affectionate creature who loves her daily soothing baths and being taken for walks around the woods. I am going to make sure this little dog gets the home she deserves, never to be allowed to get into a state like this again. A lot of Westies have skin problems as do white dogs who are more likely to be deaf too.

Some people can be cruel through neglect. Davie the German Shepherd Dog was in a terrible state when we collected him. Initially, his owner had telephoned to ask if we would take a GSD, adding that he did need a wee bit of grooming. I agreed to take Davie but said he would need to be brought to MAA because we were too busy to travel to collect him at the moment. I did not take a telephone number and so when he did not arrive I could not ring the owner to see what had happened. Fortunately, she rang again and this time we agreed that we would go and pick the dog up. I was completely shocked by what I saw. His coat was in a dreadful state and the weather was now quite hot and this had made his itchy, sore skin even more so. It was Saturday morning and we took Davie straight to the vets where they were completely shocked at his condition. The dog was sedated and myself, a vet and two other staff spent almost eight hours stripping his coat. This revealed just how sore his skin was. He was a lovely-natured, gentle creature and although he looked pretty awful, a man who

*Davie as he came
into MAA and
after a stripping*

came to visit the kennel took one look at him and that was that. Dog and man were instantly bonding in the kennel and on a walk. I have seen this happen a number of times and there is something about the instant attraction that, once seen, is very obvious. The man was able to provide me with the name of his vet and gave permission for me to telephone and get what amounted to a reference. Davie was not in the kennels long and he enjoyed the remainder of his life in comfort. There is no excuse for this kind of neglect.

Slioch, one of our resident goats, needed his coat trimmed because he was hot on those unfortunately rare hot days: he was looking like a rag bag as well. What a task! It took Graham to hang on to him and me to go round with the scissors taking off great chunks of his very thick coat, much to his annoyance. He really does look good now. He came to us as a very young kid and is very friendly. Slioch is quite a character and has been in all sorts of trouble. For instance, one night it was dark when I was closing up the chicken house, and he sneaked into our garden while I was closing the gate. Once inside, he ate everything he could get hold of, including plants that should definitely not be on a goat's diet plan. The result was a very sick goat that had to be fed gloopy stuff that looked like treacle, treated for bloating and kept in the float until he was recovered. I can tell you that he did not learn from this experience!

A lot of folk complain about the young people of today, but we have some really great experiences with them. This week, two young girls raised money for MAA, the first by preparing a leaflet about our work and presenting it before an audience in order to gain a Brownie badge. She took the opportunity to raise money at the same time and, when she proudly brought the money to us, she promised that she would become a young volunteer here once she reaches fourteen. The other young girl lives out on Shetland and, having taken a beautiful grey kitten from us, she did some baking, selling the cakes to raise money.

Adults too raise money for us, sometimes a welcome £10 but sometimes a considerable sum. Folk very often bring in items of bedding, leads, toys, coats and so on. Sometimes this stuff is surplus to their requirements, or their pet has grown out of it or tired of it, or, sadly, their pet has passed away. One of our volunteers gathers up all of this, stores it and sells it through the internet or on a stall under the name of Bella's Bargains. She works tirelessly to raise money, recruiting a team of friends to help sell. Given the right venue, Bella's Bargains can make £2,000 over a three-day period and has raised almost £20,000 in a couple of years. Another volunteer on the west coast, running various activities, has raised in the region of £10,000 over a similar time scale. MAA could not operate without the hard work of volunteers and the generosity of members of the public. We receive no funding from the government even though we are providing a service to the community as a whole.

Another income-generating venture I embarked upon in September 2018 was to produce my first book, *Folk We've Met: The Story of Munlochy Animal Aid*. This was published by Bassman Books in March 2019 and sold amazingly quickly from a print run of 1,000 books. This was a big venture for me and my friend and I spent a long time agonising over costs and how many we needed to sell to cover printing costs, how we were going to store them and so on. Once the publisher had read it, he was adamant that we should go for an initial run of 1,000 because he knew it would sell. These books have gone all over the United Kingdom and as far as United States of America and Australia. Someone came into MAA one day this week saying she had taken the book out of a local library and enjoyed it so much that she wanted to buy a couple of copies to send off to relatives. Spreading the word about a small charity like this can result in more donations and even legacies.

Week 11

We are particularly tired this week because we have a lovely Pointer in the kennels and she is in competition with Hunter, the Beagle/Cross who initiates the barking chorus, so we long for a full night's sleep. Graham pushes himself more and more with the physical work. Getting the field ready for the fete and annual dog show gives him a lot of extra work on top of all his usual tasks. This week he had even more work because we managed to get a load of firewood cheaply but, unfortunately, it was delivered so that it blocked one of the entrances to the field we would be using for the fete, so clearing that has taken up a lot of his time, so he is pretty tired. With me, it is more about mental rather than physical tiredness. I find the paperwork and the telephone calls mentally exhausting. The bank balance goes down, down, down and, no matter how hard you try to fundraise, you are never ahead. Our accountant complains that we are spending more than we bring in, but how can you not help an animal in desperate need of care – how do you say 'No'?

We have been inundated with requests for help this week from people who cannot pay a vet bill. For example, a lady phoned to explain that she was a single parent with three children whose cat had been injured and the vet wanted a £150 call-out fee because it was 6.30pm on a Saturday night. I referred her to a different vet who would not charge this much and agreed to pay. I will only know what the final bill is when the invoice comes or if the owner calls me to update me on her cat's progress.

We quite often receive rather strange telephone calls and I remember one such call that my mother took. The caller had apparently asked her if MAA wanted to take some pig swill they were wanting to donate. When I asked her what she had said, she

Slioch as a kid

said it would have been impolite to refuse but she had no idea what we would do with it. However, I was instructed to go and find a dustbin and wash it out ready to receive the pig swill. When the couple arrived they held in their arms a plastic piggy bank and had actually told her that they wanted to bring a donation now that 'the pig's full'. I told the couple that my mother thought they were bringing a load of pig swill and they were most amused and we were very pleased although I had spent a lot of time on that dustbin!

Slioch the goat had something wrong with his nose and we thought he might have something stuck inside it: he is always sticking his nose where it should not go! We called the vet out to see if he could see anything up there but could not so, since it looked like he might have an infection, he was given penicillin as a precaution. He is generally well behaved with the vet, although I did have a couple of bruises from the very hard area on his head where his horns used to be. He has been through a lot in his short life, sometimes due to his own greediness at consuming stuff a goat should not eat but also because he started forming crystals in his urinary tract and having terrible trouble passing water. As a result of the big operation, he now passes urine in the way a female goat would, but it was a choice of that or to be put down.

Because we have had Slioch from a tiny baby he is a people goat, expecting people to give him attention, fuss him and, if he is lucky, a biscuit. The other three goats came to us when they were adults, having had very little interaction with humans and they are an absolute nightmare, especially when we have to catch them to trim their feet. All male, they still have their horns which they arrived with but they do look stunning. We had them castrated because of both the smell, which comes with intact billy goats, and the fact that, especially with their horns, they can be very dangerous.

Slioch's operation was a really big operation, and, fortunately, completely successful but I worry whether or not to put an animal through something like that. It is about weighing up the experience and risks of the intervention as against the likely benefits, particularly the impact it will have on the animal. People think it must be easy for me to make decisions such as this because of the frequency with which I have to make them, but it never is easy and it has got worse as I have got older.

It has even got harder for me to make the final decision about when an animal needs to be put to sleep. One of our own dogs, Ben, is now so old and so fragile and unsteady that I suppose he should probably go now, but making that final decision is so hard since he still gets pleasure. Sometimes the decision is taken out of your hands and it is the only option left. We keep hoping that we might come through one morning and find Ben had slipped away, peacefully, in the night but I do not think we will be that lucky.

I try to make the place look presentable for the public coming to the fete by planting up pots of flowers and tidying up the yard. It is amazing how untidy this place can get. We took four loads of rubbish to the dump one day this week, as well as having a bonfire that burned from Wednesday to Saturday. We still have more stuff that will have to go next week. People are very kind and bring in all sorts of stuff that we can use around the place but a few also bring in some items, commonly pillows, that really are beyond even our use! Once, we inadvertently accepted a feather duvet and someone put it down as a lovely comfy bed for one of the bigger dogs. You can imagine the sight that greeted us in the morning.

Folk bring in foodstuff, much of which we can use and any that is excess to our requirements we distribute to food banks or other places with animals in need, but some of it is so out of date it has to be destroyed. We have pigs here and people think a pig can be fed on anything, including out of date food, but that is not the case, not if they are to remain healthy. Our three pigs, Moira, Susan and Pippa, take apples and raw vegetables along with sow rolls, which is a concentrated food for pigs, and soaked grass pellets, together, of course, with the occasional treat of a biscuit. I would not dream of feeding them out of date dog food!

We get dogs in from all sorts of backgrounds and all fed in different ways: some have only eaten human foods; some had cheap food; some only fed raw food; some with allergies and so on. We cannot have six or seven different feeding regimes and foodstuffs on the go every day, so we have one type of food that seems to cater for all needs. We use Burns dry food and all the dogs seem to get used to it pretty quickly. Although there is always water in every pen, fed through a continual top-up system, we prefer to soak dry dog food because I do not like the idea of them eating it dry and it swelling up in their tummies. Even the older dogs with very few teeth can eat it when it is soaked. There are a lot of different varieties of this particular dry food, so we can cater for those with a sensitive digestion and for puppies.

One of our own dogs, sadly no longer with us, could only tolerate eggs and potatoes and that was no way for a big dog to live. His skin would flare up and he was failing to thrive so we had to have an expensive test done which told us exactly what the dog was allergic to. I sent a copy of the test results through to the vets at Burns and, as a result of their advice, he was put onto a particular variety which, after a while, resolved his problems.

When we got back from one of our trips to the dump, we were met by the police who had brought in a very big dog that had bitten a child. The owner had been arrested and the dog was to remain in MAA until its fate was determined, probably by the courts. Once the police bring an animal in under these or similar circumstances, we are, in effect, imprisoning it and this means that without police consent neither the owners, nor their family or friends are allowed access to the dog. We have one dog here at the moment that has been in MAA for ten months awaiting the court's decision and only our own dog walkers and kennel staff can care for it until we know if it can be returned to its owner or must be put to sleep by an order of the court.

Another seagull was brought in by a member of the public. Both wings were so badly damaged that the vet said nothing could be done for the bird, so it was euthanized. We have a couple of resident seagulls who cannot fly because of wing damage but they do at least have part of their wings intact but this poor thing would have had to have both wings completely removed. If he had not been brought in, he would have been in agony and probably have starved to death, a slow and horrid end.

The RSPB Officer was in again with another kite. This poor scrap of a thing was found on the ground and obviously had been in trouble for a while since it was so thin you could have sliced bread with the breast bone. The tail feathers were not right and the main flight feathers of the wings were missing. We thought he would be dead the following morning but he had eaten everything we had put in and he has continued to eat and eat. For whatever reason, he is not perching yet, although he can be seated on a perch if we put him there, so we have put a rock into his run so that he can stand on it and hang his tail down to help get the tail feathers developing properly. He is going to be with us for a long time but, hopefully, he will make a full recovery and fly off when he is able to.

This week, we have had to do something ourselves that may seem a bit cruel. We found our missing hen under some bushes, sitting on twenty-four eggs! She, or another bird, would obviously have been laying these eggs over time, and it could have been quite a long time, but only once they are brooded would they have developed, potentially, into chicks. However, she could never have kept all those eggs warm. We took away the stone cold ones around the outside of the circle first and she was not very pleased about this. We waited until it was dark and took away all the other eggs except two which we put, along with the hen, in a box. After a night in the box, inside the hen shed, she decided she was having none of it and abandoned the two she had been sitting on. Our chickens and cockerels are a happy bunch but we would rather they did not breed. The egg raid had to be done.

Charlie Drake, the duck with a damaged wing who has been with us for some time now, is doing very nicely. However, I was concerned that we were just leaving this damaged wing with its feathers sticking up at an odd angle, so I asked the vet to take an x-ray. It confirmed that his wing had been broken badly at some point but, in their opinion, there would be no advantage in removing the part that was sticking up since Charlie Drake was managing fine as it was. I have decided not to try again to rehome Charlie, so he will stay with us forever, with his own paddling pool next to his friends the chickens and, hopefully, he will move in with them shortly.

We have had a number of dogs and puppies handed over this week. One dog signed over had killed a neighbour's cat and, obviously, there was trouble between the neighbours. He is a lovely dog and had been much loved but he is now looking for a home where he does not have easy access to cats. It is possible to retrain a dog, and we did this with one of our own dogs that was clearly a cat killer when we took him on. Through hard work and never leaving him alone with any of the cats until we were confident, he eventually became so cat friendly that he would sleep with them, particularly one of them, and accept a smack in the face from them if he got out of line. But, this is a lot of work and, for this particular dog, it is better to avoid any chance of a repeat incident.

Another hand-in was a very underweight, timid young German Shepherd. He was very nervous and, when I reached into his pen to pick up his empty food bowl, he reacted as if he was expecting to get a whack, so I was really pleased when some folk we know agreed to take him. We also took charge of a crossbreed called Dudley. We were warned that Dudley did not like people wearing hats and would nip them. I told the dog walker about the hat issue and he took out one dog to walk himself and handed Dudley to his wife to walk: she happened to be wearing a hat. I heard him tell her, 'He doesn't like people with hats,' to which she just replied, 'Oh', and began to walk Dudley. I called after her, 'He doesn't like

Robbie and his feline friend

people with hats,' and she replied, 'Oh, yes, fine', and carried on walking. The couple had got quite a long way into the wood when her husband said, 'I wonder why he doesn't like people wearing hats?' to which she replied, 'I thought you said he doesn't like people with cats!' Dudley did not nip her, although she said he kept looking at her in a very strange way.

We received three puppies during the week. The first was the most beautiful Saluki/Lurcher puppy of eight weeks old. The couple who handed it over showed no emotion, actually referring to it as 'this thing'. That same afternoon, some people dropped in for a social visit. They have had three dogs from us over the years and took one look at the puppy and decided to take it home there and then. No need for a home check because I know what kind of home it is going to. Then I got a phone call from them to say they were taking the puppy to the vet because they noticed that one hip seemed higher than the other. The vet confirmed that the wee soul's leg had been broken in three different places. My immediate response was to ask the new owners if they wanted me to take the

Kittens enjoying the sun

Who can resist this?

puppy back, to which their response was a very definite, 'No – this is our dog now.' What must that wee puppy have been through, the pain and anguish it must have suffered. But it is made for life now!

The other two Border Collie puppies came from the same litter of four. At eight weeks old, they need to be starting their socialisation training rather than having the minimal contact we can offer them here, so one is going to a MAA dog walker. The other one is going to an old customer of ours. This customer, who is a vet himself, lives in Cheshire but regularly comes up here on holiday. The family had recently lost one of their two dogs and the remaining one was missing its friend, so they popped into MAA. I just happened to show them the puppy. I knew they could not resist this bundle of fur. It will be brought back here for a visit when they come up on holiday at Christmas.

Another week passes and none of our remaining long-stay dogs have been offered homes. They are taken out mainly by the same few walkers so that they develop a relationship with them. They are loving creatures even though they are older dogs. Rocky, our long-stay boisterous Anatolian Shepherd Dog, is not old and he has three or four walkers who take him out so that he gets two good walks each day. One walker takes him into a less-used area for long walks off his lead with no problem at all. Occasionally, he forgets himself and one day this week he had a snap at one of the walkers he had not seen for a while. After that lapse he thought he would just be off for his walk with her as usual, and she was willing to take him, but when this happens he gets put straight back into his kennel to make sure he knows he has done something wrong.

We had a lovely reunion between a wee Yorkshire Terrier and its owners. The police picked it up from the side of the A9 near Alness and brought it here. The owners were decorating their house and a tradesman had left the gate open, resulting in their pet taking itself for a walk. They were quickly on the phone and, equally quickly, up here to get her back. We are lucky up here in the Highlands because I would say about ninety per cent of the police are really good at stopping and picking up a stray dog, but this is not the case everywhere. Some police are not interested, although they have a legal responsibility to take a stray if a member of the public takes it to the police station. Obviously, a loose dog can cause a major accident resulting in fatalities, so it is in everybody's interest to catch it and get it to a place of safety. Sometimes, when I am told a dog is on its way here, I put it straight on Facebook and sometimes the owners are in touch by the time the dog arrives.

Tara, our lovely GSD puppy is still causing havoc. She is in season at present and it seems to be making her even more mischievous than usual. I put my gardening gloves down for a minute and she was off with them and when I put the brush down, she dragged it off along the yard. Apart from having a wee siesta in the afternoon, which is good for a young dog, she is on the go throughout the day until she drops into her bed and sleeps through the night. She is due for spaying in November and by that time she will be old enough to be taken out on really long walks which may tire her. I never walk big young dogs very far until they are around eight months to give their joints a chance to mature.

We made the difficult decision about the dove, Eddie the Eagle, because it would be wrong to keep him as a pet, so we have released him into the woods in front of our house but leave the porch open so that he can return if he wishes. Having spent so much time hand-rearing this wee scrap of a dove it is understandable that we want him to be safe. Much to my liking, Eddie has decided he will continue to live here and is flying in and out so often, popping into the porch to chuck seed around or deposit his droppings on the lampshade. It is a good job that I am not houseproud! These comings and goings fascinate Tara and he seems to be playing with her, and certainly giving her lots of exercise. He lands on the gate near where she is, but when she goes over to him, he flaps off to a different fence and when she gets there, he moves on, eventually landing on my or Graham's head. 'Do not touch', 'Down', 'Off' and 'No' are the words Tara hears most often!

We continue working with Minty, the mother cat and her kittens. The kittens no longer hiss at me when I feed them and I am handling them every day, but mother cat remains very wary. One day this week, I was a bit late giving them their meal and she must have been hungry because she normally waits until I go away before she comes to the dish. This time she did not wait and, as she went to the dish, I gave her a gentle stroke which she clearly enjoyed until she realised what I was doing and told me to back off.

The five ferals that we took from the west coast back in June are taming down nicely. We have had an enquiry from someone who is looking for farm cats but I am very wary since I would not want to think of them returning to their feral state, especially with winter approaching. I would rather take my time with these five and wait until they are tame enough to go out to new homes as domestic cats.

Week 12

This week, a number of people have brought in items for the fete. Some will be raffle prizes, some tombola prizes but some of these items are very expensive. Donations include crystal glasses, a pretty dinner service, an antique doll and a rocking horse, so I am going to consult a local dealer to see what she says would be the best way in which we can realise as much money as possible from these items.

I got a call from someone who had heard about a woman running a small farm down south who now wanted to get rid of her pigs. The woman had filled her freezer with pork until there was no room for anything else. She had managed to sell a few live pigs until she was left with just one. However, most people do not want to take an older pig and the woman and her partner had got to know the pig, so they did not want it butchered: hence, the telephone call asking me if I would take the pig. I knew for certain that if I said 'no' the pig would go to slaughter and so it was a bit like blackmail because I knew a refusal would mean a death warrant.

So, although we had decided that we would not take any more than the three pigs we had already got, she joined them. Polly is a large black pig and when she arrived she did not want to get off the trailer and needed a lot of persuasion. When Pippa, Moira and Susan met her you would not believe how aggressively all four of them behaved. For the first thirty-six hours there was screaming, snorting and grunting. They were using their heads and snouts to push each other, but they were not going to kill. I would really not like to see what a pig could do if it chose to attack to kill. However, the relationship has quickly changed completely and they are now all sleeping together in the same arc. It will make it lovely and cosy for them all in the winter time. Polly has joined the other three in coming up to get the odd apple or ginger nut biscuit and, hopefully, we will have her for a good few years. You never really know with pigs since some become ill and die after only a couple of years and others go on to enjoy a long life. They will all be growing old together, but I think I really mean it this time when I say we have got to stop taking on any more large animals. We are not getting any younger!

Having said that, my niece, Iona, who looks after all the horses here, has wanted a Highland Pony for years. We were not going to take on any more horses, even though Iona can work wonders with any horse, even the most difficult ones, changing their behaviour in response to her manner. We had heard about a Highland Pony that had been working on a number of estates bringing the dead stags down off the hills. I had been hearing about it on and off for a while and been told that it really needed a home quite urgently now as it was surplus to requirements. So, we took the pony and Iona is going to contribute to his keep. Eventually, he will go in with the other horses, but at the moment he is separated from them by a wire fence so that they can all get used to each other.

This week, we have had to deal with a couple of birds that had to be put to sleep. One was a seagull that had been coming into someone's garden for some time but now had its tongue hanging out and necrotic. This was probably as a result of a fish hook ripping the tongue. Although the vet said it was possible for a bird to eat with a damaged tongue, it is not easy and they become very thin, so it was put down. The other bird was a crow that had both wings very badly broken and it was not fair to continue the suffering: two sad bird stories in one week.

Then we heard that the four-month-old Red Kite we successfully released a couple of weeks ago was dead. After release, he spent a couple of nights in our trees and then was tracked to Rosehaugh Estate where he remained until recently, when he moved along towards Cromarty. Suddenly, the tracker showed that he was on the other side of the firth but there was no movement. The RSPB Officer expected to find that the tracker had come off but, instead, he found both tracker and bird, dead on the shore at Nigg. The suspicion is that the Herring Gulls harassed him and forced him down into the water, so he drowned. The bird is now away for tests and analysis. So, three sad bird stories in one week is a bit too much!

A bit of good news is that the dreadfully thin kite we took in last week is doing fine, and eating well although still not able to perch. The RSPB Officer had done some research because he had previously been involved with another bird in which the tail feathers and flight feathers were not properly formed. He now thinks that it is possible that this bird is a consequence of in-breeding between closely related birds in which there is a genetic defect. So, it looks like this bird is not going to develop fully but it is enjoying its food, dancing about, perching if we put it on a perch and sitting on a rock. We are not just going to throw the towel in and Graham is going to make it a climbing box, like a staircase, so that it can hop up to the top and sit with its tail hanging down to give it a better chance of developing. This will also give it exercise and strengthen the muscles. It is a lovely, stunning looking bird and, while it is not suffering, we will take our time to decide what to do. Winter is coming and birds that cannot fly become cold and need to have somewhere they can go to keep warm, so one possibility is that we put this bird in a run at the side of the resident owl and buzzard, neither of whom can fly properly. We will think about it and try to find someone with experience to advise on this situation.

Animals are amazing in how they recover. Our twenty-two-year-old cat, Katie, who is a 'food-a-holic' went off her food and we suspected it was kidney failure. She has enjoyed a great life, never knowing cold or hunger. After a visit to the vet she perked up considerably and was back to making loud demands for her food. The noise she makes when she wants food is incredible and she has never shut up since we got back from the vets. Her meow is so loud that the vet nearly jumped out of his skin when he was examining her. Our puppy, Tara, gently pushes her nose onto Katie until she meows, because Tara seems to enjoy the sound, so Katie meows again and then Tara gives her another push to get another meow!

We often get animals in when their owners have died. It is a terrible time for the animal and when my dad died his dog, Glen, would not leave his bedroom door and never really got over the

Pigs doing what they love

loss. Quite often, when an owner dies the family do not want their pet and we end up with it. But, this week, after the SSPCA Officer brought a cat into MAA, the family reconsidered and came to take the cat back with them. Another cat, this time supposedly a stray cat, was brought in by the SSPCA Officer. I am not sure what had really happened but it was quickly reclaimed by the owner's mother who wanted the cat and it went home with her. The cat was happy to go with her so I did not ask too many questions.

We are packed out with cats at the moment and a nurse from a local veterinary practice has just brought over a stray cat that a member of the public had handed it. Then we got two more strays, one a pedigree Ragdoll, from over towards Muir of Ord, both with similar injuries as if they had been thrown from a moving vehicle. One was picked up at the roadside by a passer-by and the other one was seen beside the road but later was found hiding at the Fettes Sawmill. Using our cat trap it was captured and brought here. Both cats were terrified and absolutely starving hungry. I am speaking to the SSPCA Officer about this because it is too much of a coincidence that two young cats are found less than two miles apart, both in the same condition with similar injuries.

Another stray dog was brought in by the Dog Warden. It transpired that it got out from its home when the police forced an entry to the house in order to arrest the resident. After his release, four days later, the man came to collect his dog. A social worker pleaded his case for waiving any fees he might have incurred and I finally agreed.

The best bit of news is that Sophie, a Westie who arrived with a terrible, neglected skin condition, proved a star when she went for her recent check-up to the vet. Everyone in the waiting room was enthusing over the dog who is an absolute darling. Her previous owners must have cared about her and treated her kindly because she is happy around people and never flinches when approached, but how they left her skin to get in that condition is incomprehensible. Her skin is now soft rather than elephant hide and we have had her at the groomers and her claws cut, so she can walk more comfortably now. The lovely outcome is that the mother of one of the veterinary nurses is going to rehome Sophie, so she is made for life. Sophie will need treatment throughout her life including pills and regular baths, so it is a happy ending.

Charlie Drake, the young flightless duck, was moved into the area with the hens but decided he would prefer the next field so he could be with Glen the goose and with the goats and sheep. However, he then moved back to be with the hens and cockerels and now, he moves about wherever he wants, sometimes following Glen around and other times going into the hen house. He is a very happy, contented little duck, even if he cannot fly. He is also hanging around the car park and loitering outside the reception building because he and the other chickens can see people eating inside. There are so many birds strutting their stuff around the car park now that I am going to have to put a 'slow down' sign. It is also good to look under your car before setting off since you may find a chicken nicely settled underneath it!

Eddie the Eagle freely comes and goes all day and, when he lands on one of us in the evening, we put him back in his cage in the porch where he is safe from cats or foxes. I had not seen him for a while when Graham, who was on the roof cleaning the gut-

*Sophie looking
a lot better*

ters, phoned me to say 'Come round here, quick!' There was Eddie the Eagle sitting on his head whilst he worked. We will try our best to make sure one of our cats does not get him. Our beloved Topsy brought a bird into the bedroom one morning, so it is obvious that they will catch birds even though they are very well fed. Understandably, I was worried when I had not seen him for a while the next day. He is always sitting on a gate looking down at the cats or on a fence or a tree staring down at the dogs or annoying Tara. Then Graham called from the kitchen, 'Come and see this!'. There was Eddie the Eagle sitting on top of the kitchen cupboard, having flown in through the open window that is left open so the cats can go in and out. Three cats, fortunately the three that could not catch a cold if they tried, were sitting in the kitchen at the same time! The next day we called and called because he normally comes in if it is raining. No sign of him. We sat down in the kitchen to have a drink and worry when there was a flapping of wings and in he came, landing on my head. Eddie the Eagle tends to land on people's heads whether they like it or not, so on the day of the fete he will have to stay indoors for his own safety because not everyone will respond positively to this.

Some other good things happened this week. Arthur, the three-legged, tailless cat got a home, as did the noisy, overactive twelve-year-old cat that had failed a rehoming twice previously. Two of our noisiest dogs, Hunter the Beagle/cross and the Pointer, were rehomed and, so far, there have been no complaints, so Graham and I have had the best night's sleep we have had in a long run of sleepless nights.

We also heard from the Edna Smyllie Fund that we will be getting £3,000 towards our new tractor but, unfortunately, we have to buy the tractor first, send them the receipt and then we get the £3,000. Hopefully, the offer will not have a short time limit on it because there is no way we have the money needed to buy the tractor yet, so it will mean a lot of fundraising. I will do a couple of other grant applications to see if we can get the money sooner because our old tractor has really had it. Once we get the 'new' tractor it should be our last big spend for quite some time since we have recently replaced the heating/cooling system and the industrial washing machine and done a few other major renovations on the kennel and isolation block.

But we could have ended this mixed emotions week with a major disaster. Graham was working with the old tractor in the field, either putting on or taking off the bucket, and something was not happening that should have been happening. The weather was really hot, so I decided to take him out an ice lolly from the freezer. He asked me if I could just pull a lever down for him, so I did, and it juddered and shook but in the wrong direction! He let out a scream and yelled to me to pull it the other way but I got in a panic and did it the wrong way again. He was screaming so loud that neighbours came running across the field. I managed to pull the lever in the right direction and he got his hand out, doubling over as the sweat just poured off him and he went absolutely grey.

The old tractor
on its last legs

He would not let me see his hand and wrist initially as he cradled it against his body, probably because he did not want to look at it himself. At first someone was saying we should call an ambulance and then my brother-in-law wanted to take him to hospital and not wait for an ambulance. I could see by his face that he was in absolute agony, and he is not someone who makes a fuss, but he refused to go to hospital. When we looked at his hand and wrist it was a real mess. His hand had two big indentations in it and his copper bracelet had pressed into his wrist, but he could move his fingers so he reckoned nothing was broken. His hand swelled up to nearly double its size and we put it in a bucket of ice cold water which, along with some painkillers seemed to help. He could not use it for a while and our neighbours were wonderful, pressing home offers of help with anything and even hanging a door that they knew he was about to do before this happened.

We will never forget that accident, Graham because he thought he was going to lose his hand, and me, because of the thought that I had done this to him. If we needed any further encouragement to get a new tractor, this was it. I have told Graham that I am never, ever helping him again if it has anything to do with that rusty old bucket of a tractor. I do not think he will actually ask for my help again!

Week 13

This week, there have been so many requests for financial help from people who cannot afford a vet's bill. It is frightening me because none of the requests are what you might call 'cosmetic'. All of them relate to animals in serious need. Yesterday, I was contacted by a woman whose dog has a dental abscess and the vet told her it will be in the region of £400 and she has no money at all. The vet would not do it without confirmation that she could pay. She was crying on the phone and, you know yourself the kind of pain a dental abscess causes, so I had to say we would pay. Yes, I can hear some readers saying, 'If you can't pay a vet's bill, then you should not have a pet,' but circumstances change and people do not always do the most sensible thing. However, this woman did have two dogs and another caller had four dogs, so some people really do need to sort themselves out and be realistic, no matter how much they love animals.

The population of the Highlands has increased so much since the year 2000 that there is an ever-growing need for the kind of help MAA has to give. Whilst there are a number of areas classed as areas of multiple deprivation, there are plenty of folk on very low income or unemployed who seem to slip under the radar. We are a small charity, always running at a loss and really not in a position to keep paying other people's bills but it is the animals that are suffering and they suffer in silence. At the moment, the People's Dispensary for Sick Animals (PDSA) have no free hospital up in the Highlands and very limited opportunities for people to get subsidized veterinary treatment. I hope to be able to talk with them to see if there is some way that they too can support people who are in real financial need and genuinely cannot afford to pay for veterinary treatment.

We have had a wee girl working here on work experience. She has been an absolute joy. There was nothing she would not do and she did everything with a smile. She could see what needed to be done and used her initiative, getting on with whatever was needed. She cleaned kennels, walked dogs, and it was her luck to be here when there were a couple of puppies, so she got to give a lot of cuddles. Not all our young helpers are as sociable and co-operative as this wee girl and sometimes they hardly speak to the staff or volunteers, but she was a joy and is planning to become a vet. I always have a chat to the youngsters when they start working with us, telling them what is expected, explaining where everything is, and letting them know it is all right to ask as many questions as they like. After one particular youngster had been here nearly a week and did not seem to be enjoying her placement she complained to her work placement supervisor that there was no toilet available, so I make a point of showing them all that we really do have one and they are welcome to use it!

We had some more good news this week. A poor wee Jack Russell was picked up at Dornoch. It was very cold and very scared so we warmed it up, fed it and put its photograph on Facebook. Success! Facebook is proving to be a very useful tool for us because as soon as I put something on it, the word spreads and is passed on and on and, in this case, within a very short space of time the owners had been alerted and were here to collect a much relieved Jack Russell. How would we have managed before the internet?

We also got a home for our long-stay old German Shepherd Dog called Clyde. He was spotted by some folk looking at dogs in the kennel and after they took him for a walk they were smitten by him. Clyde has a lovely nature and after a failed rehoming he returned easily to his usual kennel behaviour. Unfortunately, this behaviour involved him standing for much of the time, watching intently what was going on in the other kennels and who was coming and going. He was happy enough and enjoyed his food and walks but, at his age, he should have been resting. He will definitely put on weight once he is established in his new home because he will relax. The next day, I spoke to the lady who took him home and she said he was sleeping in front of the stove on his big new dog bed and looking very comfortable indeed.

For some dogs, kennels is like heaven. They are kept clean, fed, exercised and kept warm, all as part of a routine, which dogs appreciate. There is a lot going on for them to see, so they are never bored. They begin to feel safe. I have been into some of the homes our dogs come from and they are dirty, chaotic and the animal is not fed or exercised regularly. We have even had dogs in that have clearly been given drugs, and not those prescribed by a vet! Ask any of our walkers and they will tell you that most of the dogs are eager to be taken out for their walk and they enjoy sniffing and looking at whatever is in the fields, but as soon as the walker turns around to return to the kennels, these dogs speed up and the return trip is completed in far shorter time. If life in the kennels was awful, they would not rush to get back. Mind you, they do realise that when they get back there will be a nice meal awaiting them! We do sometimes get a dog that does not want to go back into their pen when they get back, but, once inside and given a nice treat, they quickly settle. No dog ever goes to bed without a second meal in this place and when we start the evening cleaning and feeding round, they are all up for it.

We have started taking some of the dogs to a secure area of open ground that is specifically for dogs to be off their lead. It is possible to book this area for sole use and so we can take almost any of the kennel dogs but it does mean putting them in a car to get there. We have taken some of the oldies and long-stay dogs, including Cooper our very long-stay deaf dog, and they thoroughly enjoy it. We have taken one of the dogs, Jason, who is very destructive in his kennel, just to get him tired out. We included one of the dogs that has been with us for ten months awaiting a decision from the court as to whether he has to be destroyed. We can guarantee that he cannot get out from the enclosure and he loves racing around, playing ball and being chased. I have written to the court to say how this dog has changed and what a nice dog he is now. In total, we took seven of them all at once this week and they had a brilliant time. They were all flat out in their beds when we returned. I have now made a block booking for weekly access to this secure area so that we can do this every week. It would be nice if we had an area like this close to the kennels but although we have a lot of land it is all occupied by sheep, goats, horses and pigs so we cannot close off an acre or so.

The Red Kite is doing well and eating whatever he is given. However, the RSPB Officer has now confirmed that this bird will never be able to fly because neither the tail feathers nor flight feathers are ever going to develop. We are going to have to decide what we do with this bird. Although we have a few birds here that cannot be released because, for a variety of reasons, they would not be able to hunt for their food, we have now said that we will not keep any new bird that will never be able to fly. It goes against everything that is natural, but this beautiful young bird loves his food and is thriving, so what do we do? We will have to make a decision but I want to do a bit of research to see if we can find anyone with experience of his genetic problem. At the moment, we have space for him and kites are solitary birds so he is not missing the company of other kites so there is no immediate rush to make the decision. It is not going to be easy.

Unfortunately, a wee pigeon was handed in that was too young to have left its nest. Even though I managed to get a feed into it before I went to bed it was dead by morning. You are more likely to have a successful outcome if you can get these wee things as soon after whatever incident has befallen them. If you can then get some antibiotic into them and a feed you stand a better chance of them surviving but you cannot win them all.

Arthur, the three-legged, tailless cat is in his new forever home and doing really well. He has the company of a dog and three other cats. He has a lovely nature and is a real rogue, getting up to all sorts of trouble. He enjoys using their climbing toys and a missing leg does nothing to stop him getting around. He is not being let out yet but I am keeping in touch with the owner to see how this big softie gets on.

A man from near Strathpeffer telephoned in a dreadful state, having lost his cat. It was a young, healthy cat and he had looked everywhere for it. I felt that, given the cat's age and the location of the property, it was more than likely that the cat had got shut in somewhere when it had been nosing around. It was a very relieved man who telephoned back that same day to say the cat had been shut in a shed and was back with him now. I knew how he felt because one of our cats, Topsy, disappeared after a neighbour's cat had been a bit nasty to her and she is a sensitive cat, probably with a bit of Siamese in her makeup. I could not eat, I was so distraught and I could hardly speak to anyone. We searched and searched, calling and calling and then, when it was dark, we found her under the shed not more than a few yards from the house. She was taking no notice of our calling and it was just pure chance that Graham got down and shone a torch under the shed. She would not come out until she was ready. One of our other cats, Tillie has to come in at night before Topsy can go out because Tillie chases Topsy! In fact, all the other cats chase poor Topsy because she is so sensitive and rather aloof – you could say she is a diva! When she goes into the kitchen she treats the other cats like they were commoners and she is far superior, hissing at them even though the kitchen is their territory not hers. She will not allow them in her territory which happens to be our bedroom.

Moira, my mother-in-law, has been working flat out all week baking in readiness for the coming fete. Her baking is very popular and we get advance orders for the cakes, especially her carrot cake. However, I bought the wrong type of custard powder (how would I know!) and it caused a custard cream disaster, so I was not popular. But, when I got back home an old customer of ours who had recently lost her dog visited and took a Westie/Yorkshire Terrier who, spookily, looks just like the dog that had recently passed away.

To end the week, I almost had some very good financial fortune. I had to go to the bank to put some money in and get some money out for the floats for stalls at the coming fete. It took longer than expected because the machine that counts the money was not working and the teller, who was new, had to count it himself. When he handed me the receipt he had put a digit in the wrong place and instead of it reading £840 it read £8400. When he asked me if I was happy with everything I assured him that I was, but then asked him if he was also happy. When he replied 'yes', I said that if he was happy then I was very happy indeed, but he obviously picked up on my body language and tone of voice. Unfortunately, he suddenly saw what was amusing me and changed it back to £840. Shame!

Week 14

What a week! It is the week of the fete, our annual big money raising event and the weather has been getting steadily worse all week. The forecast was diabolical. We have never called it off for reasons of the weather or anything else, so we were not going to call it off this year.

It all began over 30 years ago when myself, my mother and a couple of other ladies set up an organisation called K9CATS with a local vet on our board. It was purely a charity that raised money to do neutering. This meant that we were trying to raise money for K9CATS and for Munlochy Animal Aid, holding charity auctions in local halls and so on. After a while it was getting too much being so closely involved with two charities and some of the active members of K9CATS were getting older and some passed away, so we spoke to the Charity Regulator and it was agreed that if K9CATS was closing, the money from its account could be transferred to MAA since it was serving a similar function.

Then I thought, why not have a dog show with a few stalls around the place? I had seen it be successful in other places and it was an instant success here. We were not making the kind of money we make at the fete nowadays but it was good money for then. We did not open until 2pm in those days and the place would absolutely be heaving with visitors dead on 2pm. The queue of traffic trying to get in for 2pm was right back to the A9. The police would come to control the traffic, and a police car would park at the end of the road to try and control the flow. One year they gave us our own traffic warden to manage the parking. We began buying up gazebos whenever we saw one come up cheaply and sometimes were given one. Ideally, we would have a big marquee so that we could have all the stalls in one place along with the teas, so folk could sit out of the rain, but these cost a lot of money.

Preparation for the fete goes on for weeks before but it really hots up in the few days leading up to it. We try to make the place look reasonably tidy and pot up plants so that the entrance looks good. We even borrow plants from Munro's Garden Centre, just for the day. Many people contribute towards the fete, some baking, and some making sandwiches, some helping with any last minute bits of repairs and so on. There is a general buzz around the place and lots of people call in with donations for the bric-a-brac or raffle and with money donations if they are not going to be able to join us.

As if we did not have enough to do, Tara, our GSD puppy, suffered from a sore leg just before the fete. The way she rampages around, it is perfectly understandable that she would have a sore leg at some point. However, having recently lost another GSD to cancer, and remembering how it had started with a sore leg, I was desperate to get her seen by the vet. It was almost impossible for the vet to make a thorough examination since she rolled around on the floor, flinging her legs in the air and not co-operating. He did the best he could and ended up putting her on some anti-inflammatories. They seem to have worked so it was probably just a sprain.

By Friday, the weather was giving us a sample of what was to come, but we still had to clean the toilets, set up the café area, give the barbecue its final clean-up and we decided to put up a trellis to shut off the four pigs from looking into this area. Last year, Pippa Pig stood behind the fence, intently watching the burgers being cooked and, more importantly, the bacon burgers! She certainly did not look like she was affronted that we were cooking her relatives: her expression was much more like, 'Any chance of me having one of them, please?' Now we have four pigs we did not want any gatecrashers.

Eddie the Eagle, our baby dove, helped Graham by standing on top of his head while he worked and Tara recovered enough to 'help' by grabbing at the hose pipe while I hosed down the yard. This hosed me down along with everywhere else that we would rather have kept dry.

When we awoke at 6am on Saturday, the rain was torrential. We

This goat was not amused at being temporarily relocated

have to get all the gazebos set up on the morning because it just cannot be done the day before. We tried one year to set up on Friday evening but, remembering these are old gazebos intended for occasional garden use, their legs are frail and on the Friday night the wind rose and so did the gazebos. We lost four that year so we have never done it again. We also have to evict the sheep, goats and Glen the goose from their field so that we can put the car boot sale in there. We suspected the weather would put folk off paying their £10 to sell from their cars but we could not take the chance, so the animals had to move. All went well except for one Shetland Sheep who refused to leave. She resisted being cornered, captured, persuaded or anything else. In the end, after the air had turned pretty blue, we recruited another sheep and our very tame goat, Slioch, to help us usher her to her temporary quarters.

The downpour continued and it was the worst weather we have ever had for the fete in all those years. However, folk got so wet that after a certain point they stopped caring and just carried on! Cakes sold, tombola went, bric-a-brac sold, burgers and teas did really well, perhaps because you could wrap your hands around something warm. Some of the volunteers running stalls found

Let it rain!

their hands had got so cold and wet that they could no longer pick up the smaller coins and were happily comparing who had the reddest, and in some cases the bluest hands! Of course, you have to remember that gazebos like the ones we use accumulate water on the roof and unless someone gives it a good prod with a stick to let a controlled stream of water come down, it will eventually bring down the whole side of the tent with disastrous consequences. Cars and vans got stuck in the mud and our old tractor earned its keep by pulling them out.

The dog show carried on, lots of dogs dressed in rainwear like their owners. Some dogs that had never had raincoats before were bought new ones from Bella's Bargains, a stall selling pet products that had been donated to MAA. A large, cross-looking curly haired dog was standing nose to nose with a small mongrel who was attempting to shelter under his owner's umbrella. The owner said they were talking to each other and saying, 'I would much rather be indoors on the sofa, wouldn't you?' In the midst of all this, a stray dog was brought in and then an injured seagull.

We certainly did not have as many visitors this year and I thought we would be lucky if we made £1,000 but the final total was £8,500, the raffle alone bringing in £4,500 thanks to all the really attractive prizes donated. The first prize was a cabin delivered and erected by Fettes and who would not want another shed! People, though wet, were actually having fun, as were most of the dogs, and there was no quarrelling between humans or dogs. We

Tara enjoying her jigsaw puzzles

saw members of the older generation as well as youngsters splash-
ing in muddy puddles just for the fun of it! Later in the week we
were even getting donations from people who said they just had
not felt like coming out in that awful weather, so they donated
what they might have spent.

All the usual feeding and cleaning of big and small animals still
has to go on, even though it is fete day. The evening rounds up in
the kennels have to be done and all the animals made secure for
the night. The gazebos need to be dried and taken down and any
remaining items from our stalls have to be put away in the dry. We
got to bed around 12.15 on Sunday morning, having been up since
6am.

I awoke at 7am with a splitting headache, a sore throat and a
runny nose, so not in the best of moods. More cleaning and tidying on Sunday as well as the usual routine. Tara was a great help
when she found four jigsaw puzzles in a box which she emptied

and then ripped open, scattering the contents i.e. 4 x1.000 pieces, around the yard. As I tried to sweep the pieces up, all sticking to the floor because it was very wet, she helped by grabbing the broom and running off with it. The poor seagull had died over night but the stray dog was collected by its owner.

I was so tired by the end of that day and still with a raging headache. We took five of our own dogs for the last relaxing walk in the wood. I tripped on a wet tree root and, I am ashamed to say it, I did say quite a few swear words: so, there I am swearing and the five dogs rushing around making a lot of noise. At that point Graham shone his torch a little further forward only to reveal a very tiny tent with three bicycles outside it. They must have been terrified and we called out, 'Sorry', to which they replied, 'OK', but they sounded petrified. This is the third time that we have come across a tent in the wood at night. Worst of all was the night we were walking about 11pm with our dogs and, at that time, they included a beautiful white GSD called Sammy. Sammy was fine with us but he could be quite aggressive to other people and we had given him a home because nobody else would. Dogs, when they come across something that scares them, can either back off in fear or go into full attack and Sammy never backed off. I was praying that nobody stuck their head out of the tent or called out before we could get hold of Sammy.

Once the fete is over we get back to normal. Wee Sophie the Westie who had the dreadful skin condition is doing brilliantly but the vet does not want her to go just yet to the new home that has been arranged for her. So, Sophie will stay with us for a while yet. She has another general health check next week and then she is already booked in to be neutered the week after. Her skin was so badly infected that they have to be sure there is no infection when she is operated on. In the isolation block she was getting a bit fed up since her only company is a very unruly Border Collie who spends his time throwing things around his pen, including his bed. She loves her walks so we are arranging for her to get extra walks and she has been moved into the main kennel block so that she can see all that is going on. She is loving it. Her tail never stops wagging and she is getting quite cheeky, begging treats from people and grumbling at some of the noisier dogs.

The poor little Ragdoll kitten that we trapped at Fettes Sawmill is still very very nervous. Goodness only knows what had happened to her before we got her. She is eating well but has definitely never been housetrained since a litter tray is completely alien to her. She is still covered in sores which the vet thinks are friction burns and has broken teeth. She is very reluctant to come forward for any human contact. She is kept in a large crate at the moment, albeit with a view of the car park so she can see chickens and people wandering around and there are other cats in the same room so she can hear them meowing. Cats by nature are clean and she is really very dirty in her habits. You get cats that will not use wood-based cat litter and others that will only use earth or gritty litter but I have tried it all and she simply uses the bed or floor. We have someone who is very interested in having her, and has others of the same breed, but he knows he would have to keep her confined for a while. If her litter tray remains close to her bed she will eventually choose that in preference to her bed.

I do wish people would let me know the outcome of their visits to the vet. A young woman telephoned me to ask if MAA was able to help because her pet insurance would not cover an ear problem that her predominantly white cat had. She had taken him on after his previous owner had passed away but he already had an ear problem. Now that the problem is worse, the insurance company will not pay for its treatment. The fact that he is predominantly white suggests he may have cancer of the ear because a number of white cats suffer from this. In the end, I agreed to pay but have heard no more from her and will probably only know what the outcome was when I get the invoice.

Another trip to the vet was for a cat that was due to be rehomed. She started vomiting up blood but it turned out that she had been retching so much, trying to cough up a fur ball, that she burst a blood vessel. Apparently, not that uncommon. We rehomed one of our cats to a lady who had lost both her husband and son and then her dog and, understandably, she was desperately sad and in need of a companion. The cat we chose was a gentle creature that will sit on her lap and enjoy being stroked and petted, so he has got a good home.

Two of our hens are both claiming ownership of a wee black

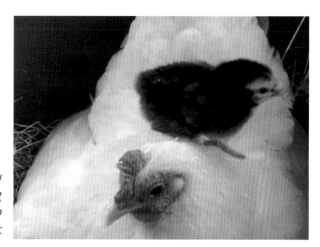

One mummy claiming ownership of her chick

chick. They will take turns with it under a wing and will sit with it between them while they chatter away to each other. If we try to pick up the chick, or even touch it, they are quite aggressive so we have not tried to sex the chick. I am hoping it is not another cockerel but, if it is, there is no way I could let it go because the two mummies are so attentive.

Week 14

We have had a dog in for a few weeks that is called Michelangelo but we call him Mikey. He is a nice Staffordshire Bull Terrier who likes people but he is very reactive to other dogs. Some folk came in and decided they would like to take him on and so, after a home check, off he went. I warned them about his reaction to other dogs but they did not seem fazed by it. However, Mikey was returned the next day since they had not quite realised just how reactive he was. They did the right thing because they realised they had made a mistake and just could not cope with the way he reacts when he gets into close proximity to another dog.

There are too many dog-related incidents now involving both children and other animals. The number of dogs that react badly to other dogs has increased noticeably. Some of this can be put down to the fact that people take on a dog when they do not have the time to train it properly or they leave the dog alone too much because they are working all the time, ending up with a frustrated dog. Some folk take one on because they like the look of it or it is a status symbol but they do not consider the characteristics of the breed. One popular television series resulted in lots of Husky type dogs being bought but without consideration of the size they end up and their strength or exercise needs.

We get a lot of dogs in here that have come from houses where drugs are being used and the owners are really not focussed on the needs of their dog. Dogs thrive on regularity of meals, exercise and sleep. Sometimes, we have taken a dog that has ingested drugs and it takes time for us to get these out of its system so we can see the real character.

Our own wee Jack Russell, Judy, is nearly blind now and is thought to be around seventeen years old. She is a law unto herself and was in kennels for a long while. She was brought in by the SSPCA from the east coast and was wearing a muzzle, which we were told was apparently very necessary. Her poor face was raw in one place where the muzzle had rubbed. That came off the day she came in and the only time she wears one now is for a visit to the vet, as a precaution. She does have an attitude problem and can be very snappy and will nip people, unless they are offering food! Nobody wanted to give Judy a home for obvious reasons, although one of our volunteers became very fond of her and would take her out for long walks on the beach.

Then one day a lapse in concentration on the part of a couple of dog walkers ended up with Judy being attacked by another one of the kennel dogs and it was a bad attack. She was saved only by the quick thinking and bravery of another dog walker who pushed his own hand inside the mouth of the big Akito that had grabbed hold of her. This surprised the Akito and she let Judy go: she had to be rushed to the vet, returning back with stitches. We moved her in with us for a bit of post-operative care and she has never gone back to the kennels. The Akito had not shown real aggression to other dogs before this incident although she had played a bit rough on a couple of occasions. She was very successfully rehomed and, as far as we know, has been behaving herself.

Judy has various problems including tummy trouble, so we try to be careful what she eats. She is the worst dog ever for begging at the table but we try to be strict with her. She particularly chats Graham up at breakfast because he has a cooked breakfast while I only have cereal. So, we are very careful with her fragile tummy and we know what she can and cannot eat but she does like cat poo and this really does upset her digestion! You can always tell if she has indulged in cat poo because she tends to burp afterwards and the smell is dreadful. Even now, Graham and I can give her a stroke and a bit of attention when she wants it, otherwise she will make it clear that she is not in the mood and we do not push our luck.

She has never been a dog to wander but because of her eyesight she can get herself into situations that she finds difficult to get out of. This is the second time that she has gone missing when we returned from the late night walk now the nights have drawn in.

Volunteers at the street fayre

We did not immediately realise that she was not with us and the other dogs when we got back into the yard and we called and called but no response. The way to find her is for me to go up to the kennel block and make a noise which will set the resident dogs barking: this will always set Judy off in response, so we were able to locate her still in the wood at the back of the house. No more walks off the lead for Judy!

Eddie the Eagle also went missing for one night. Graham went out with the usual dish of food expecting Eddie to land on his head and come back into the porch with him, but no sign of Eddie. He really seems to like coming in at night and especially so if it is raining. The next day, he came into the porch in the afternoon so I shut him in earlier than usual just to make sure he was in for the night. His latest escapade was to get in the pick-up truck with Graham and to travel on his shoulder. I just want him to stay safe. He is such a joy to us and I worry that when something is such a joy it often goes wrong!

Our presence at the Dingwall Street Fayre was such a success. We brought home £1,428.98p which included a donation of £500 from one individual. We had such a lot of positive comments from people about the work of MAA and lots of folk came to tell us about the animals they had taken from us and the joy they had brought. We had taken a truckload of items, many of which had not sold at the fete the previous week, and quite a bit of this I thought we would be taking back again at the end of the day. However, one person's junk is another person's treasure and this proved to be the case. Graham and I, along with some volunteers, had a bric-a-brac stall, a tombola and a baking/produce stall, all of which were really successful. The plant stall was less successful probably because most of the plants were dying back and it looked like we were trying to sell dead stuff. I also sold seven copies of my first book, *Folks We've Met*, which was very pleasing.

On the way home from the street fayre we called in to collect an injured pigeon from someone. Unfortunately, the poor creature did not survive despite us giving it antibiotics and steroids. It is so important with birds to get them examined and treated as soon after the incident as possible and then to put them somewhere quiet to recover. Once infection sets in and the bird goes into shock it is unlikely it will survive.

Cat is a very rude word around here at present. Every spare space is full of cats at the moment. We are endlessly cleaning litter trays, feeding them or taking one or other off to the vet. We have just taken in another five very feral kittens that were found in a hole in the ground over by Invergordon. They had to be trapped after their mother was killed on the road. I did a very stupid thing when I wormed and flea treated the first three that were trapped: when the other two were caught I put them in with their siblings but realised they all look alike and I do not know which three had already been treated. I will just have to wait a suitable time and do the lot of them. Tiny though they are, they are ferocious, hissing and spitting but they will come round eventually when I have got the time to focus on taming them. Today, for example, I have got a few bits of paperwork that must be done so I will bring them into the room and let them get used to human company. Because there are five of them, if one of them kicks off then the others start and it is like five balls of fire erupting, so I am going to split them up.

The Ragdoll kitten trapped at Fettes Sawmill has gone to a lovely home. The couple have other cats including a Ragdoll and when the chap came in to see the kitten he was absolutely smitten. She is a very timid cat and we have only suspicions concerning how she got into the dreadful state she was in but she will do well with this couple, especially since there are older, established cats in the

Taming the wild ones

home. I was really pleased that just before she left she actually approached me for a stroke when, previously, it had been me who had to approach her.

Minty, the mother cat, has now been neutered and separated from her kittens. She is enjoying getting all the food to herself and being able to relax without her kittens. Although the people who originally brought her to us were willing to have her back as a feral I have decided she will stay with our feral colony. She can live out her life in relative comfort, with no worry about getting food, a nice warm cat house, a play area where she can climb trees and, if she feels inclined, enjoy the company of other cats. We will introduce her gradually, using a big crate initially, and then she can either mix or be on her own as she wishes, but with no more pregnancies and someone to monitor her health for the rest of her life. Of course, I still have the slightest hope that she might suddenly tame down and then I could get her into a domestic situation. Her three kittens will get homes as soon as possible.

We have a beautiful English Bull Terrier in kennels while his young owner is not very well. She absolutely adores this dog and asked if she could come in to see him this weekend. She stopped to buy him a nice steak pie on the way and she clearly wanted to have the dog back but was equally clearly not able to do so now nor in the near future. The dog has been in and out of various kennels all its life and we talked about what was best for her and for the dog. He is a lovely rogue of a young dog, full of enthusiasm for any activity, and that is no life for him and is a constant concern for her because she really loves this character. I put no pressure on her at all and suggested she go away and think about it. I made sure she realised that there was no rush. After she thought about it, she finally saw the sense in letting him go to a new home. We have now got someone who is particularly keen to have this breed and is travelling some distance to visit him shortly. It is heart-breaking but better for both the young owner and her dog.

The kennels is full again this week, but there is a flow through. Dudley, the dog that could not stand people who wore hats, has gone to a nice home with a hatless family. We are doing very well down on the east coast of Scotland for rehoming. This is because I have taken out adverts in the *Press and Journal* newspaper and sent in pet portraits. This resulted in a man and his daughter coming over to collect a lovely but nervous Border Collie who had to get on with his cats. The dog was a very nervous character but the new owner was so gentle and patient when they were introduced that it was clear that the dog would be fine. I do not mind paying for adverts if it can be shown to be effective.

I so wish we could find homes for the remaining long-stay dogs. A couple of people have shown an interest in Speedy the Lurcher. His pal, now called Monty, lives happily in his forever home but Speedy is more of a problem. Poor Cooper, our deaf long-stay dog, has had no offers of a home for the past two years. He is a difficult, highly strung dog, possibly because of, or just made worse by, his deafness. His original owners had been given him as a present, not realising he was deaf and he had started biting. I was reluctant to take Cooper on originally but although it is very slow, progress has been made. We are taking him each week to the secure park where he can be let off his lead and he is loving it.

Lucky, one of our dogs awaiting a court decision as to his future, has been waiting a very long time and now will have to wait longer because his owner failed to turn up at court. I will probably have to write another letter of support for this nice dog that has changed so much since he has been with us.

Week 16

We still have not decided what we should do about the kite that was brought in five weeks ago. We have debated this long and hard and I think we have come to the conclusion that we will have him put to sleep, although he eats heartily. I honestly do not think it is fair that a bird that not only cannot fly but also cannot even perch is kept alive. Both the owl and the buzzard that we have kept for six or seven years can fly a wee bit but not enough to be able to survive in the wild, although they thrive here. The two resident seagulls can at least flap around a bit and have a swim in their pond, getting daily visits from other passing seagulls. These birds are all at least using their wings and do what birds are meant to do, but this poor kite cannot. For a bird of prey like this to live his entire life on the ground is unnatural.

Although we have plenty of space if we were to keep the red kite, unless he was in a covered enclosure other birds might attack him because they see him as vulnerable. He is not taming down at all and this reinforces the fact that this is a wild bird of prey living a very unnatural existence. We have no way of knowing what is going on in this creature's mind, nor how stressed he really is by living like this. This has forced us to think more generally about whether, in the future, we would keep any bird that came in without one or both wings. Some of the vets now are inclined to say that if a bird needs invasive surgery, such as losing a wing, that bird should be put to sleep. We are waiting to have another word with someone who is knowledgeable about red kites before we make our final decision. I really do not like making this type of life or death decision.

I am trying to find the most suitable setting for our smelly hedgehogs. They need to find a space big enough for the big one, called Pudding for obvious reasons, to root around but warm enough for the wee one, Hoggy, to be comfortable. Pudding is big enough to hibernate outside and I could release him but they are company for each other and they are happy stuffing themselves with an unbelievable amount of food. Nobody who has not had the pleasure of the company of hedgehogs would believe just how overpowering their smell is!

Eddie the Eagle is Graham's constant companion. No matter what he is doing, Eddie is on his shoulder or his head. When Graham goes into the cat enclosures Eddie cannot come, so he sits outside on the windowsill watching what is going on. Even if Graham is repairing something and swinging a big hammer, Eddie still sits on his shoulder not budging. A couple of times this week, Eddie has been missing and when it gets to bedtime, Graham is out there calling and holding up food to entice his friend back into the safety of the porch for the night. He was missing for a whole night and part of the next day but then turned up again. We have noticed that there has been another dove coming around and he might have found a friend, but I might get a ring put on him so that it is easier for people to spot him. Of course, we do not know that Eddie is a male and she could be Edwina, so who knows what the future holds.

From time to time we have paid for an animal to avoid it having to go back to its owner. This is a very rare occurrence but this week we did 'bribe' an owner to let us keep their dog. I had been alerted to the fact that this person had been trying to sell the dog over the internet and then someone contacted us to say the dog had been sold and then, apparently, resold again by the buyer. The next thing that happened was that the SSPCA brought a stray to us and I recognised it from the description I had been given. This poor creature was 'doing the rounds' being sold and resold and clearly not cared for because he had been straying. For the sake of the animal, we offered to buy it when the owner arrived to retrieve it and it went out very quickly to a loving, forever home with some folk we know.

We also rehomed two dogs that came from Wales! Their owner had been trying to find someone to take them and could not even get a rescue centre to find space for them, so we agreed to take them if they could be brought here from Wales. It was a long drive but they arrived, none the worse for it, and were really gorgeous, finding a home together very quickly. The owner was much relieved that his efforts to responsibly rehome his pets had paid off.

We managed to reunite an owner with a dog that the SSPCA officer brought in one night about 10pm. His owner was really pleased to get him back and it turned out to be a friend of a member of our family, so we will be able to hear how the dog gets along. This dog had been imported from Spain and had a bad skin condition. It had only been in this country six weeks and its current owner was not the first owner during that six weeks. A number of these dogs being brought in from overseas have had to be put to sleep because of health issues. Under the circumstances, I contacted the Animal and Plant Health Agency (APHA), a government department responsible for safeguarding animal health for the benefit of people, the environment and the economy to alert them to yet another animal being brought in with health issues.

We have had to have another Border Collie put to sleep. The history was that, despite having lived with a caring family, including children, it had, for the first time in its life, bitten someone and it was a bad bite. Something about the dog had changed suddenly and nobody could explain what had happened. The dog was far from easy to handle and there was something wild about its eyes. We managed to get it to be seen by a vet, using a sedative, so that he could see whether there was any reason for this change in behaviour such as a bad tooth, an abscess, a tumour or whatever. The vet could find no apparent physical reason for the way the dog was behaving and it was behaving very aggressively.

In the kennel block, the dog was really difficult to deal with and it managed to bite someone who was very used to handling and walking dogs. This was not a nip and he really meant business. Nobody wanted to walk the dog and I had to make sure that the staff did not enter his pen unless he was secure in the outside area. I have seen a lot of aggressive dogs over the last forty-one years but this one was really something else and the only thing we could think was that there was something happening in its brain. If we had gone for a brain scan and it had revealed a tumour it would

*Part of the
kennel block*

have meant major surgery with no guaranteed positive outcome and would we have ever got a home for it? It was far from easy getting this dog from the kennel to the vet for the final journey and we ended up having to use the catching pole to keep a controlled distance between us and the dog and then into a crate. This is fortunately an incredibly rare necessity. Much as we love dogs, we cannot risk someone getting a serious injury. I had to telephone the original owners to let them know what had happened and it was a very sad conversation. This is the second time we have had to put an aggressive Border Collie to sleep in just a couple of months.

On a more cheery note, the second cat that was picked up some weeks ago at the roadside, with broken teeth and wounds suggestive of having been thrown from a moving vehicle, has found a good home, so that is both of them gone since the Ragdoll was rehomed last week. But, as if we did not have enough cats at the moment, a very pregnant cat was handed over and gave birth shortly after arriving. This is not a feral cat and will be able to be rehomed and so will her lovely little kittens. Graham has every reason to panic because I want every one of them but especially one little female that is unbelievably friendly! Graham is pleased that two of them are already booked to lovely homes with folk on the waiting list and this is despite the fact that the people have not even seen these kittens yet.

Polly, the newest addition to our pig family, has been causing problems. There has been a lot of pushing, quarrelling, snorting,

The kindly cockerel caring for two new bantams

and squealing and so we decided to temporarily separate her from the other three by installing an electric fence in part of their enclosure. It was a waste of time because the shock was not bad enough and they simply barged through it, taking it down and breaking the wires. However, we need not have bothered because everything has settled down and they are all the best of friends again. They have two big arcs to sleep in but they are all sleeping in one of them, all together again. Maybe one of them had come into season and maybe they get grumpy when this happens but I am no pig expert. Hopefully, this was a one off occurrence and we will not have to move Polly to another area.

I took delivery of another eight rescued hens from down south. These are all barn hens and so they have feathers and are giving us eggs already. In fact, my friend Cathy went down south to collect them and one of them managed to lay an egg in her car on the homeward journey! It is astonishing how quickly they have settled into their new home with all the other chickens.

Week 17

One day this week, Graham and I noticed a dreadful pong in our kitchen. Now, I know that most folk would not consider it very hygienic to have a cat litter tray in the kitchen but we have one cat that does not think she should have to go outside, especially if the weather is less than inviting and she might get her feet wet. However, we clean the tray as soon as it is used and we sniffed it, reassuring ourselves that the smell was not coming from there. Graham and I were so busy during the day that we did not have time to institute a search until just before bedtime at around 11.30pm. We looked behind cupboards and even took a torch to look behind more inaccessible places but still could not find anything unpleasant. The pong was everywhere and then we managed to narrow it down to one spot: that is, Bunty's igloo bed! We tried to entice her out with food but she refused the offer, so Graham had to firmly but gently haul her out. We had found the origin of the smell – it was Bunty's backside! Clearly, she had at some point in the day had diarrhoea and, being a long-haired cat, she was carrying around the after effects. So, at nearly midnight we showered her rear end with great difficulty since she is a very sensitive diva who is against any kind of grooming and especially washing. Bunty is a very lazy, fat cat, despite the fact that we do not give her treats as we do with Topsy, who is a skinny rake, or Katie, who is very old and has an overactive thyroid and is allowed to eat anything she fancies. Bunty has been checked by the vet just in case her pudding shape is caused by something nasty but, no, it seems she is just a fat, lazy cat, so she is going on a diet!

Bunty and Tillie are 'kitchen cats' because the kitchen is their end of the house along with three other cats, whereas Topsy is the 'bedroom cat'. Not only do they quarrel if a 'kitchen cat' ventures

114

Bunty as she arrived at MAA and as she is now

into the 'bedroom cat's' territory and visa-versa but they cannot meet outside. When we go to bed we make sure all five of the cats who live in the kitchen have come back in from the garden where they are free to spend their day. This means that I can let Topsy out at night, which is her preference. However, this particular night we had been calling and calling for Tillie to come in. I went to bed and mentioned to Graham that we cannot let Topsy out because Tillie is still out. However, about 5am Topsy starts scratching at the bed-room window because she had woken up and wanted out and she can be very insistent. In my sleepy state, I just opened the window and almost immediately the screaming started when Topsy met Tillie! Though Tillie returned, Topsy took off and it was nearly midnight that day before we managed to get her back indoors. Not a mark on her, but we had been so worried that she may be somewhere badly injured.

One morning this week, the police arrived with a poor wee dog in their van. A workman had discovered it lying beside the road and thought at first that it was a fox. Despite the fact that the dog's coat was really dirty, including flea dirt, he covered it with his jacket and called the police. I was really concerned by the look of the dog and took it straight to the vet who could find no injury, but it was very underweight. The SSPCA officer came to look at it and was as concerned as I was. Then we got a phone call from owners who were looking for it and told me that they had got the dog from MAA when it was eight weeks old and it was now seventeen. They assured me that it was much loved and attended the vet on a regular basis. They even gave me the name of the veterinary practice so that I could confirm this, which I did. Some of the dog's condition could be put down to age and various chronic problems but I was concerned by the fleas and how it had ended up cold beside a road at 7am. However, the dog was very pleased to see them when they collected it and they were just as pleased to see the dog so you cannot always tell just by looking.

A man telephoned to say he had taken his dog to the vet and the treatment had cost £250 which he had been able to pay. However, the treatment had not worked and the vet now wanted to try a different treatment and this would cost £450 which the owner just did not have. After the caller explained his circumstances, we agreed to fund some of the costs. Various vets send in their invoices each month and this month MAA has paid over £3,000 in veterinary fees, much of this spent helping folk who cannot afford to have essential treatment for their pet. Once a payment has been agreed I need to be able to get in touch with the vet who will carry out the treatment as quickly as possible since the longer the delay the more pain and suffering for the animal.

The very sad news this week was that we received a call saying there had been a fatal road traffic accident on the Black Isle and the wee dog that had been in the car with his mistress had run off. We took the dog trap over for the SSPCA officer, who lived close by, to use if she needed it and discovered that the lady who had died had been a very good friend of ours and a friend to MAA for many years. A lot of people went out looking for this dog but he was not recovered until the next day. This lovely couple and their wee dog, Rusty, featured in my first book, *Folk We've Met* and her death has cast a shadow over everything. She will be very sadly missed.

Week 18

It has been quite a good week for rehoming dogs. The SSPCA brought us two young Border Collies that had been used for breeding but were not good for working and so were surplus to requirements. They were lovely-natured dogs and everyone who came into contact with them fell in love instantly: needless to say, they went out quickly to new homes.

The English Bull Terrier that was signed over to us by his young owner a couple of weeks ago has been rehomed to folk over Aberdeen way. They are very keen on the breed and thought he just looked so beautiful, although not everyone would agree! We even managed to find a home for a six-year-old Newfoundland who had also been used for breeding and was handed in by her owners. She went to a new home with people who had not had the breed before but just fell in love with her because she really was very cute, if rather slobbery. They understood that six is quite old for the breed and they will only have her for a few years. Even the man who comes here selling fish has decided he wants a dog, so I am on the lookout for the right one.

Sophie, the wee Westie who came in with such an awful skin condition, has been neutered now after weeks of extensive treatment and has gone to her new home down in Carnoustie with the mother of one of our local veterinary nurses. Sophie is an inspiration to us all when you consider what she has been through and still remained such a loving, gentle creature. She has been no trouble at all, no matter what treatments she has had to endure.

Another dog that stole all our hearts was a gentle good-natured Border Collie called Gem who was no longer able to work. Her coat was so neglected that her ears were fixed by matted fur to her head and her tail was one heavy, solid lump of matted fur and her bottom was in a dreadful state. The staff here did what they could to make her more comfortable but I managed to get a local groomer to see what she could do as a matter of urgency. She shaved off the fur from her rear end and removed the mat from her tail, the mat coming off in one lump full of grass seeds and bits of stick and left no fur at all, just a sore on the tail. She has a couple of lumps near her nipples so she is booked to go into the vet next week and while having the lumps removed she will be neutered. A lady I have known for thirty years or so is going to take Gem into her home to live along with her other three dogs. They have all been out together two or three times and she fits in perfectly, so much so you would think that Gem had known them all her life.

Our own Tara continues to be an outrageous puppy, never stopping throughout the day until she absolutely drops. She was so tired one day this week that she flopped down on old Ben's bed in the kitchen and could not keep her eyes open. At that moment, Katie, our twenty-three-year-old cat, decided she too wanted to use that bed and she pushed and pushed at Tara until she had managed to get enough space to settle herself. Tara just could not summon any more energy to push back or chase Katie, so they just slept. Mind you, Tara is not the only one of our dogs who can be mischievous: the alarm on my phone no longer works properly since Moss, one of our Border Collies, who is now sharing our bed, chewed it!

Our cat situation is just starting to calm down. We ended up with seventeen feral kittens from various sources and it has been a continuous, exhausting round of feeding and cleaning as well as finding the time to try to turn these furious little bundles of fur into sociable cats suitable for rehoming. Feral kittens need a lot of time spent getting them used to being handled and played with if they are to stand a chance of getting to a normal domestic life. They are very clean and learn quickly to use a litter tray. I think I have got homes for fourteen kittens and young cats, including one of the kittens that came in with its mum, Minty, a couple of months ago. We really need to get about twenty cats and kittens away to homes for us to get our lives back since it has been so exhausting.

Our members of staff are such an asset. An incident this week shows how dedicated they are to their work here. One of them injured her knee whilst bending down in the kitchen and was in tremendous pain. The pain was so bad that she was shaking and crying and, once we had got her onto a chair, I telephoned for an ambulance. The paramedics arrived with a doctor and managed, gradually, to manipulate her knee back into a position where she could straighten it, then stand and finally put weight on it. I was all for her going off duty right then but she insisted on remaining to the end of her shift and because we had lost time sorting this out, another member of staff, who should have gone off duty, said she would stay until everything was finished. Despite me telling her to take the next day off to rest her knee, she was back on duty for her next shift. That is dedication. One good thing that came of this is that the two paramedics decided they would like to come back and walk dogs!

On one of our many trips to the vet, we discovered a pigeon in the road that kept falling over so, obviously, we took him into the vet as well. He thought the bird had been attacked by a cat because it had a wound under one wing so it was given antibiotics, put in a box and brought back here. Fortunately, a member of staff has an aviary and offered to take care of it until its tail feathers grow back and it can balance properly as well as fly.

Biggie and Brindle, two of our longer-stay residents, did not seem to mind being apart after all. I did not think we could ever split them up because they came in together and could not bear to be apart for any length of time. However, I took them for a walk, off their leads in the wood and then back to separate pens for the first time and they were fine. The very good news is that they both got homes this week, so separating them was the right choice. Brindle, the younger of the two has gone to a local family. Biggie, who is just the most adorable 'smiling' dog, has gone to be companion to a lovely lady who is a relative of mine who lost her husband a couple of years ago and then lost her old dog a few months ago. The new owner came in along with her son and Biggie endeared herself instantly by stroking the son with her paw.

Eddie the Eagle is almost permanently attached to Graham now. The only place he does not go with him is to the toilet, but that may change. They ride in the tractor together and even when Graham is using the awful machine that cuts through walls, creating dust and dirt everywhere, Eddie is still on his shoulder supervising proceedings. If Graham is not available, Eddie will favour me with a visit but I, who hand reared him, fed and washed him morning, noon and night, have now had to take a back seat in his life.

Week 19

Around twenty dogs and their owners attended an animal blessing on a lovely calm, rain-free Sunday. The controversy continues over whether animals have souls and so on but the Reverend Canon Melvin Langille is very sure that they do and they stand as much chance of going to heaven as we do. Any animal can be brought to the blessing and we have had guinea pigs and rabbits as well as cats, dogs and birds, but this time it was all dogs, and all well behaved ones! He blesses each animal and sprinkles them with holy water and then he goes into the kennels and blesses the current residents. It is another bit of stimulation for them so they enjoy it. He also blesses all our other animals such as the sheep and goats, chickens and even Glen the goose, who is much less likely to bite nowadays than he used to be.

There was one very large Newfoundland at the blessing who was not so much interested in the blessing compared to the food which his owner had stocked her pockets with, but it kept him quiet. Eddie the Eagle put in an appearance but got bored after a while and flew off. In fact, Eddie has been absent on the odd night, coming back early morning in time for his breakfast, so he is obviously out on the razzle! The tea tent was well supported that Sunday and we raised £180 from donations.

We have a lot of hens and cockerels now and they are wandering around the car park and kennel block all the time. The dogs are so used to seeing them that they are not that bothered but one day there will be a disaster and one of the chickens will get killed. We are having to make a sign asking folk to drive slowly once they come off the road because the chickens and Charlie Drake, the flightless duck, are sometimes rather slow to get out of the way. They are all used to people and people mean food! The cockerels are all different and absolutely stunning to look at and the chickens approach people who can pick them up because they are so used to people. Poor Charlie was visiting the vet this week because he developed an eye infection so is on eye drops twice a day for a week. He charmed everyone in the vets and within a couple of days the eye was showing such an improvement. He still has his private pond in the field: it is actually a huge plastic dog bed filled with water but it gives him all the opportunity he needs to paddle around if he wants.

Hoggy, the baby hedgehog, has also been seen by the vet because he was a wee bit snuffly and developed a small swelling on his nose. The vet cleaned it up and was not sure what it was but thought it might be a skin infection like mange so they have sent off for some medicine suitable for a hedgehog. Personally, I do not think it is an infection because Hoggy has been here too long and he is kept very clean and Pudding, his companion, has not got any infection so it certainly is not infectious. It has not stopped Hoggy from eating his usual quantity of food and he and his pal are still in the house despite their awful, overpowering smell. They are both now of a size that they could be released into the wild and hibernate for the winter but they have had such a sheltered existence that I feel it would be better to wait until spring and let them start their wild life from then. We still do not know if the pair of them are male, female or one of each but, even if they are a male and a female, we have never had a 'captive' pair breeding in all the many years we have had hedgehogs in MAA. If they did breed and produce gorgeous baby hedgehogs, everyone would be thrilled, especially since I would not have to be the one feeding them.

We were hopeful that someone might be interested in taking Cooper away with them. The reader may recall that Cooper, our deaf border collie, is our longest resident and not an easy rehoming prospect. The person who was interested seemed to be perfectly placed since she lived alone in a somewhat isolated rural setting and worked on her own, so Cooper would make a great companion. However, she learned that her job was about to change and she would not be able to take Cooper with her to work. One day we will get the right home for this boisterous rogue of a dog, perhaps with someone who has previously managed a deaf dog and has the patience to train Cooper, and they will need the patience of a saint. We still have our other long stayers, Speedy the Lurcher and Bobby, the corpulent old gentleman, but they get plenty of attention from walkers and kennel staff and the two dogs that are waiting for a court to determine their fate are still waiting to know if they have to be put to sleep.

Michelangelo, the Staffie who was rehomed and returned a few weeks back, has gone to a home where they absolutely adore him. They know how reactive he is to other dogs and they are sensible people who have taken precautions to make sure he cannot get out from his garden and is not off his lead where he might come into contact with other dogs. The dog that was handed over some weeks back when it had killed a neighbour's cat has also gone to a home with no cats, no neighbours with cats and a very high fence all around the property. Both Michelangelo and this dog were gentle easy dogs to love and are apparently fitting in beautifully with their new families who are making the necessary compromises.

The flightless kite is still here, eating well but still unable even to perch. Next week, we are seeing a vet who has knowledge about birds and birds of prey in particular. If he says there is no hope, regardless of any treatment, that this bird's quality of life can be improved, then we will ask him to put the bird to sleep straight away.

We still have a lot of cats and kittens but we are managing to tame a number of the feral and semi-feral youngsters. Several weeks ago when someone who was looking after a large number of semi-feral cats passed away, we took five of them. At first we were not sure whether they would end up going in with our other ferals, which would not have worried them since they were used to living with many other cats. However, Graham has spent a lot of time working with these very attractive young cats and they are still being tamed but it is obvious that they will be suitable for a domestic setting in the not too distant future. Another one of Minty's kittens has been rehomed this week and the others are ready to go since they tamed down really well. My great joy is that Minty is now much more amenable to human company and this has been a long, slow and careful process. She even enjoys playing

Tilly
Trotter

with cat toys now, although she does not always remember to play with her claws retracted, so we are looking to rehome her in a domestic setting rather than put her in with our other ferals. Real cat lovers are often happy to take these cats that need a lot of time to settle in and the new owners need a lot of patience since it may be some time before they will do anything but come in for food and use a litter tray. Eventually, they will be found settled on the settee snuggled up with their owner, but it will not happen on the first day.

Our own Tilly was ferocious when we took her in from a local garden centre. Her kittens were easier to handle and would climb up our arms but she would spit and hiss. Eventually, she realised she was missing out in this arrangement and she became more and more tame and is now one of our own 'kitchen cats' and the sworn enemy of Topsy, the 'bedroom cat'.

Week 20

This was not a good week. I am so exhausted from feeding and cleaning so many feral kittens that I have developed a raging headache, backache and a stinking cold, so I am worn out. Then my sister, Alexis, passed away after a long illness. Her passing was expected but that does not make it any easier for those who have loved her. Alexis worked with the cats at MAA for over thirty years and was amazing when dealing with feral cats because she had a gentle, quiet manner and they felt safe with her. A couple of days after my sister died we had to have our dear old dog Ben put to sleep, so I am really down at the moment. Our staff have been great in taking on as much responsibility as they can, just to give me and Graham a bit of time to deal with all the family stuff that has to be done, and to have time to grieve. However, there is no such thing as 'compassionate leave' for us when it comes to running this place and no matter how we feel, we have to keep going.

So, you can imagine that I was not terribly overjoyed to hear that we were going to get another six feral kittens from a couple of different litters found behind Tulloch Castle Hotel in Dingwall. With winter approaching it is important that we manage to trap them and the Cats Protection League are helping us do this using cat traps. We trapped two and then another two, one of which is a gorgeous looking ginger tom but as wild as a tiger. This particular cat is around five months old and I have no idea how we are going to get it to the vet to be neutered since you could not put your hand anywhere near it, even with gloves on. I am going to talk to someone at Aigas Field Centre who is very knowledgeable about Scottish Wildcats to see if he thinks it is worth having it DNA tested. It has so many of the physical characteristics of the Scottish Wildcat. Obviously, it is not a pure wildcat but a hybrid, so I will

Minty

see if he thinks it is worth doing the test. Most of the wildcats around now are not one hundred per cent pure, even the ones in the captive breeding programmes, but they are gradually improving the gene pool, trying to get back to the pure Scottish Wildcat.

Four of the kittens are really cute to look at but ferocious is an understatement. One of the ladies helping to trap them was badly bitten and had to go to Raigmore Hospital and I got mauled by a real cutie that inflicted bites and scratches across my hand. I bathed my hand in something that stings a lot, so it must be doing some good! The kittens from one litter are only around ten or eleven weeks old and I am already able to touch one of these kittens. With feral kittens, I split them up so that I have them in pairs. Having six ferocious kittens all hissing and spitting makes it much harder to tame any of them and they copy each other, whereas in pairs there is usually one that is more amenable to taming and that helps the other one tame down. This has been the longest spell ever for having to cope with feral kittens and I am praying it will calm down soon. When we see the last little tail going off down the road with a new owner, I think I will crack open a bottle of champagne, even though I do not like the stuff!

After 10.30 one night this week, a woman telephoned to say I had got her two Cocker Spaniels and she wanted to come and collect them. I explained that I had not had any dogs brought in today but she insisted that the police had told her that a man had taken her dogs to MAA. She told me that she wanted to come and collect them now and was clearly so sure that they were here that it took quite a bit of persuasion to stop her arriving. I was not sure what was really going on and whether this was some sort of domestic dispute or whether the dogs had been picked up as strays by this man the police referred to. She was clearly very distressed whatever the cause. In the end, I promised her that I had her telephone number and if two Cocker Spaniels were brought in by anyone, I would ring her no matter what time it was. She has not been back in touch, so I can only assume that she has them back. We have had folk banging on our doors and windows early in the morning and late into the night, demanding their dogs be handed over to them when we have not had sight nor sound of their pet.

Being such a popular holiday area, it is not uncommon for holidaymakers to lose their dogs. This happened to a couple who were holidaying in their campervan with their much loved English Bull Terrier. Whilst walking him in a local beauty spot he took off, probably getting the scent of a deer or hare, and had not come back. The worrying thing was that the dog was wearing a collar and a harness and could easily have become tangled up and unable to get free. They relocated their campervan from the campsite to the car park at the beauty spot and a number of people helped them search for their dog. It was three days later that he was spotted and recaptured and they said that the state of the harness suggested he had indeed been stuck somewhere. So, that was a happy ending with one very hungry and thirsty dog reunited with desperate owners. Even dogs that are well trained can become confused when they are in unfamiliar territory and just cannot find their way back to their owners nor their vehicle. It might be better to keep them to lead walks but, if off their lead, definitely take off the harness and collar so long as they are microchipped. The thought of having to go back from a holiday without the lost pet is unbearable.

Sometimes, we have quite rare breeds of dog handed over and

this week we got a Dogue de Bordeaux signed over for rehoming. This breed is a large French mastiff and one of the oldest French dog breeds. It is a massive and very powerful breed that is known for its loyalty and courage but rarely lives beyond eight years. They also need a lot of grooming despite being a short-coated breed because they have folds of skin that can become sore. They also tend to slobber quite a bit. This particular dog is a young dog, very expensive to purchase, and the owners had only had it for a few months when they realised that they could not give it the exercise it needed. We had a couple of this breed handed in before and found them good homes so I was hopeful and, sure enough, this one was rehomed very quickly too. It is a breed you either love or hate.

Graham and I have registered as dog handlers/restrainers with a company that provides a dog control service. Our role is to go to a property where officials need to gain access but where there is known to be a dog within the property. The dog might be really friendly or it might be very aggressive, so we go along at the appointed time to meet with the officials so that we can manage the dog whilst the officials do whatever they have gained entry to the property to do. We have already been called to a couple of situations and will decide after a few more experiences whether it is something we want to continue being involved with. Whilst it is another source of income, we are there to try to reduce stress for the animal but there might be situations in which we can help the owner if, for example, they are being evicted. Under these circumstances we could offer to take the dog into kennels whilst a situation is being resolved.

We rehomed a lovely friendly cat this week but, within a couple of hours of him going to his new home, he had gone out through the cat flap that they had forgotten to lock. Unfortunately, he is still missing at the moment but he will turn up at someone's door so, hopefully, they will get him back and remember this time to keep windows, doors and cat flaps secured until he is fully settled in with them. Many years ago, someone took a beautiful Lurcher bitch from MAA and, despite the fact that they were familiar with the nature of the breed, they let her off the lead for a run up on the moors a day after they took her. Despite many people going searching for her for a long time, she was never found and to this day it is a mystery what happened to her. When someone takes on a new pet it is essential that they hope for the best but anticipate the worst and take absolutely no risks until they are very sure of the animal and no matter how experienced they believe they are as owners.

Another West Highland Terrier is in the kennels. She was picked up by a member of the public who initially contacted the SSPCA who advised her to bring the dog here. The dog was really dirty with a gummed up, mucky eye; terribly neglected ears; a filthy coat; sores and faeces around its bottom; and claws that were so long that they were curling sideways, making it almost impossible for the animal to walk. Kindly, the woman and her partner arrived here at about 7pm and we scanned the dog but it was not chipped. I was quite horrified by the terrible condition of the creature and the woman was really pleased that we were showing so much interest in its condition and that I was going to get it to a vet the next day.

The next day, the dog's owner telephoned explaining that it had been a relative's dog and she had promised to care for it. However, in her current circumstances, she could not afford vet bills and could not get any help from the PDSA or anyone else. She wanted to provide care for the dog but Westies can be high maintenance and she did not have the time since it required such a lot of attention. Apparently, she did have a tube of eye ointment but she did not use it because the dog growled at her. I explained to her that she was an old dog and was going to need regular medication for the eye and ears and, under the circumstances, would she like us to take the dog, deal with its veterinary needs and get it a new home. I also pointed out that, because of the condition in which the dog was found, I would have to notify the SSPCA so that they could keep a check on how the dog was being cared for in the future. I hope I managed to make this sound like an offer of help and not a threat. I asked her to think it over and to telephone me the next day to let me know what she wanted to happen. Her wise decision was to let MAA rehome the animal. Penny, as she is called, is now looking much better after a bath and must be a lot more comfortable. I think I have found old customers of ours who will come and see Penny, talk to the vet who is treating her about ongoing prospects, and maybe decide to offer her a forever home.

We see all sides of human beings here. We meet fantastic youngsters, volunteering in their free time, joining in community activities and making plans for their future. And then we see young people who are physically and mentally wrecked by drugs on a downward spiral of a lifestyle. Often, they love their pets but are not fit to care for themselves let alone a dog or a cat: we end up with the poor creature here whilst the owner gets more and more caught up with drugs and all that goes with it. Sometimes, the owner manages to get out of the cycle and take their pet back but it is so hard for them and quite often it is better for the animal to be rehomed until the owner has sorted out their life, sad though it may seem.

Week 21

It is the best bit of news we could have: Bobby, our very long-stay resident, has got a new home. Poor old chap has been in kennels for over a year and everyone has become very fond of him. One of the walkers has walked him for two to three hours, spread between two walks, every day but Bobby is a portly gentleman who sometimes chooses to sit at the side of the road and watch the traffic for a while. The walker has developed a really good relationship with him and has taught him to sit and give his paw and to be a bit less reactive to other dogs. We never give up hope of a home for a dog like Bobby because he has a lovely nature and a couple came along who fell for him immediately. It really does often happen just like love at first sight. They took him for a nice long walk and, by the time they came back, they were kissing him and he was kissing them, so it was a match made in heaven. They did, as a parting shot, point out that Bobby would be losing a wee bit of weight in their care! We have since received a photo of Bobby in his new home, laid in his bed with a new toy. What a lovely ending after a very sad beginning because Bobby came here when his owner died and he remained in the house beside her for some time.

The funny thing about this particular dog walker is that he takes on the difficult-to-home and long-stay residents and they always get a home on his watch, so he has now taken on Jason, a rather energetic Border Collie who was wrecking his pen. They go off on a three-hour walk each day and Jason is so tired that he is even lying down in his pen rather than hurling himself and everything else around. There was one Staffie that had been in for a very long time and this walker developed an enviable relationship with the dog. Once rehomed, the new owner brought the dog back to visit and the reunion between ex-walker and dog warmed your heart. The dog was as pleased to see his ex-walker as the ex-walker was to see the dog and they cuddled and nudged each other, both making soothing, adoring noises.

One of our regular walkers decided to take a very large, strong dog for a walk in the wood this week. She is well able to manage big dogs like this but got an awful surprise when the dog caught sight of something and bolted with her walker in tow. When you are walking dogs you are constantly on the lookout for anything that might spook them or entice them to give chase but, on this occasion she had no warning. We have no idea whether the dog saw a deer or a squirrel or whatever it was but she had the walker on the floor and dragged along on her knees before they came to a bank and the walker was able to get a bit of leverage and come upright again. To her credit, she never let go of the lead and had no intention of doing so, no matter what. However, it did tell her and us that this particular dog was too strong and is better suited to the couple of strong male walkers who usually take her out.

We always try to match walkers with suitable dogs and some walkers can only manage smaller dogs, older dogs or dogs that do not lunge. We give the walkers any helpful information about the dog they are taking for a walk: for instance, some dogs, particularly some of our Border Collies, walk beautifully on the lead until they see a car or a bicycle, so they are best walked on forest paths and not on the road. We have a selection of different types of leads and harnesses so we select whatever gives the walker the greatest degree of control and the greatest comfort for the dog. We have one dog at the moment, a Lurcher called Speedy, that is best suited to wearing a muzzle when out because he would dearly love to fight with any passing dog but when prevented from doing so, he will nip excitedly at his walker. I dislike seeing any dog wearing a muzzle but sometimes it has to be, but just for a specific purpose and a short time.

Gem, the Collie who came in with a dreadfully neglected coat, went off to be neutered and had a mammary strip because of the lumps we noticed. She has now gone to a lovely home with three other dogs and her owner has already sent us photos of her looking absolutely beautiful and very happy. Penny, the fourteen-year-old Westie, has also gone to her new home. Her potential new owners very sensibly talked to the vet who had been treating her while she was at MAA just to make sure they knew what they were taking on. For instance, the eye ointment that Penny will need for the rest of her life costs £70 a tube and the eye drops are £27. She will always need bathing and ear care because of the dreadful state her skin was in, but the new owners were not deterred and collected her on Monday. Happy endings are so important, especially when there have been a run of very sad cases.

Speedy, our long-stay Lurcher, and Cooper, our long-stay deaf Collie, have both been spending time in the enclosed safe park down in Dingwall, running around like mad things, and are loving it, coming back tired out. Unfortunately, in their excitement, they had a wee quarrel this week and needed to be parted but no harm was done. If only someone would come along and foster them that would be another happy ending.

Our own Tara, the GSD puppy, has been at the vet because she had an upset tummy for a couple of days. The problem is, you can never tell what she has eaten when we have been walking her and our other dogs in the wood and she would quickly scoff whatever she found in order to stop the other dogs getting her tasty morsel. It was a new vet and when she saw this huge hurricane bounding into her surgery she asked if Tara needed to have a muzzle on. My reply was to tell her Tara was a real muppet and adored people but she was just a bit boisterous – an understatement. The vet could not find anything wrong with this rampaging puppy that is going back in a couple of weeks to be spayed. Whatever it was causing the problem, it has gone through her and she is back to normal.

Hoggy and Pudding, the hedgehogs, have moved out of our house at last and we can breathe fresh air again. They have moved into one of the pens in our isolation block at the back of the kennels. The pen they are using has underfloor heating but the edges are not heated so they have a choice of warm floor or not. They have now been joined by one of the two new baby hedgehogs that came in last week and they are all getting along fine. The other baby hedgehog unfortunately died in his sleep, possibly from pneumonia since he had been outside in such terrible weather. We

A poorly hedgehog

can only do what we can do and we do not know how long he had been outside in the cold and wet. Anyway, the three of them look very cosy in their big pen and take surprisingly little notice of each other. My only concern now is that Hoggy and Pudding are not eating as much as they used to and I wonder whether some kind of body clock is clicking in and they think they should be hibernating. If this is the case, Hoggy and Pudding will have to come out of the heated pen.

I am still hopeful that the cat that went missing through an unlocked cat-flap within two hours of arriving in his new home will be found because he was a lovely friendly cat. He is microchipped, the registration being to MAA, so we should hear if he is picked up but as the weeks go by it is looking less likely and I am wondering whether he has met with a fatal accident. Facebook has its uses and one of them is that any animal that goes missing anywhere in Scotland can be put onto it and this results in lots of folk looking for the animal or recognising it as belonging to someone they know.

Fortunately, the chick turned into a hen

There were six strays dogs brought in on one night alone this week and three of them were reunited with their owners that evening. Getting through to the microchip company is so frustrating and, admittedly, the lines are probably very busy but it does not make it any less annoying when a dog is brought in by the police or a member of the public around midnight. Ideally, I would like to ring the microchipping company, get the contact details of the owner, and then telephone the owner to say your dog is safe and you can pick it up tomorrow morning but it is just not as quick and smooth as it could be.

We have not had time to even start to erect the second-hand barn we bought over the summer and that is a pity since it would have been such a useful place to put our machinery and yet another place for some of the animals to go at night. But we have acquired a lovely brand new shed adding to our very large number of sheds. No sooner was it up, and an electrician had fitted the electric supply so it can have heat and light, than it was full of rabbit hutches containing feral kittens. This means that the last four ferals could be moved out of our house and into the shed. However, this lot are not taming down as quickly as I had hoped. The last three or four weeks have been very full on, what with family mat-

Might this be the daddy?

ters to sort out, so I have not had as much time as I would have liked to spend with the kittens. However, I am able to stroke one or two of them and although they still hiss and spit, they accept a stroke. I have them in pairs in the hutches and once one of the pair starts to enjoy being stroked and starts to purr, the other one sees that it is missing out and will come round eventually.

The ginger tom that looks so like a Scottish Wildcat remains really ferocious and I have yet to talk to the person up at Aigas who is involved in the captive breeding programme to see if he thinks it is worth having a DNA test done when we put the kitten in for neutering. We have a special cage that we can use when it is impossible to handle a cat. This small catching cage is put into the crate the cat is in and we manoeuvre the cat into it and this enables the vet to sedate the animal without anyone, including the cat, suffering any injury and reduces stress for the cat.

The black chick, hatched by two hens seven weeks ago, has, thankfully, turned out to be a hen since we really did not want another cockerel. I will let her and her two mums out today so they can mix with all the other chickens since she is big enough now to cope.

Eddie the Eagle has stopped coming in every night and stopped spending most of his time sitting on Graham's head. We now see him on the cherry tree or on the telephone wires but with a companion dove, so Eddie, or maybe Edwina, has chosen a more natural lifestyle. We know it is Eddie because when we call, he puts his head on the side and he will fly into the cherry tree and look down on Graham as if to say, 'I'm fine!' We are still leaving the outside door to the porch open every night even throughout this terrible weather, just in case he wants to come back, but he has made his choice.

The Red Kite has been put to sleep. He was eating everything he was given but there was nothing of him and his tail feathers and wings were just the same, so there was no progress despite giving him a few weeks to develop. He lacked any muscle tone because he could not use his wings and he could not jump up to perch. When the vet tested his reflexes they were really poor so we decided it was time to let him go and it was done with speed and the minimum of stress. His condition is the result of inbreeding and so there are bound to be other kites born with this same genetic defect, but they simply may not have survived.

It would make me very happy if I can get a bit of time to tidy up the paperwork. I try to be as organised as possible, paying bills straight away and filing everything so I can keep the accounts up to date and ready for inspection any time. We are always classed as 'late' putting in accounts but I don't think we are alone in that. However, the only way to do this is to shut myself in a room and lock the door and turn the phone off, but then something happens and I have to come out, so it all gets put on hold again. I am determined it will be finished by the end of November because that is when I need to start doing the Christmas letters and cards which are such an important way of keeping in touch with all our wonderful supporters.

Week 22

The friendly cat who was lost on his first day in a new home has, I am glad to say, turned up so all is well but the second of the two wee hedgehogs that were handed in two weeks ago has now passed away. Minnie, as we called her, had started to sneeze and snuffle a bit which could have been due to worms or pneumonia, so we also wormed Hoggy and Pudding, with whom she shared a large pen in the isolation block. However, she was dead one morning this week. The weather has been so awful that I suspect she had been out in the cold and wet for quite a long time before she was picked up and brought in, just like the other tiny hedgehog that came in at the same time. Because of the thick frosts on the ground at night they had probably not been finding the food they needed. All of this, and her size being so small, conspired against her and her immune system was probably very week. It was really disappointing because she looked like she was going to survive even though she was very small for the time of the year. But it was not to be. My concern was growing because Hoggy and Pudding were not eating as much as usual but they seem fine and I really think their bodies are telling them that they could and should be hibernating. No sooner had Minnie passed away than we received another very small hedgehog and so we are keeping this one in a crate in a warm shed on his own so that we can monitor how much he is eating and keep a close eye on his condition, especially since we do not want Hoggy and Pudding to pick up, or pass on, anything that is contagious.

I felt really sorry for a woman who telephoned for advice. She and her partner had been travelling home at night when they saw a deer that had, presumably, been knocked down. It seemed to be able to move its legs and so they picked it up and put it safely in some bushes at the side of the road to recover from a knock on the head or shock. However, when they went back the next day it was still there and still just alive. She was terribly upset at having left it overnight. It was too far for Graham and me to be able to get there quickly and so I advised her to contact a local vet or the police to ask if there was a gamekeeper or someone with a gun licence who would come and end the distress it must have been suffering. Apparently, she paid for a vet to attend the scene and put it to sleep. There are kind folk around!

We got a terrible shock one day this week when we arrived back to see my niece flagging us down because an ambulance with flashing blue lights had turned into the kennel car park. As we pulled in, we saw that the dog warden's vehicle was parked and my first thought was that the warden had been mauled by a dog. At that point, another ambulance car with flashing lights arrived and by that time my heart was pounding so much I thought that I would become the casualty. However, it transpired that they were at the wrong address and should have been at a neighbouring property. In fact, the neighbour had only been ringing the out of hours service because her pain prescription had run out and she was suffering pain, but in the middle of the conversation her phone went dead and the call centre assumed she must have suffered a heart attack, hence the arrival of the emergency services. All's well that ends well but what a fright!

We still have ten 'old' feral kittens and two 'new' feral kittens. We got a call from friends who live a few miles away and they had spotted a mother cat with a number of tiny kittens following her along the road. The cats crossed and went into a garden. However, the man who owned the garden would not allow my friend to go in to find the kittens. We left here straight away when she rang and took a couple of trap boxes and food. We searched around and were concerned that there was a very deep ditch full of water and a very narrow bank of grass right on the roadside. The owner of the property refused to allow us to set the trap on his land so we had to put it on the grass bank, not an ideal spot from a safety point of view. We spotted two of the kittens, that looked to be about seven weeks old, and had got themselves stuck between some bushes and a fence. Graham managed to make a grab for

A rescued fawn

them and caught them both so we popped them into a box. We could not see the rest of the kittens so we brought the two back here and then returned with more food.

A neighbour came out and chatted to us and then the owner of the garden came out and said, 'Well, you are nothing if not determined', to which I replied, 'Yes, we are *very* determined.' He then told us that we were wasting our time and would never catch them. He could hardly believe it when we said we had already caught two of them. I have been back and forth to see if I can spot them and a friend of one of our dog walkers lives near there and is keeping a look out for them. All we wanted to do was to set the catching boxes just inside the garden – we were not planning on holding a party in his garden nor ruining his plants – so I have no idea what his problem is. The two we have caught are coming around already, playing with members of staff who have toys and will tame down nicely for rehoming. Being as pretty as they are, with huge eyes, will make their chances of a home far greater. We will not give up since, with winter coming on rapidly, they are unlikely to survive.

Two of the feral cats who live in the cattery are no longer with us. Graham knows these cats so well and recognised that one of them was poorly, especially when it allowed him to pick it up, so it had to go to the vet who put it to sleep. The other elderly feral was found dead in his bed one morning, so that was a better end. But, worse still was the lovely wee black feral kitten that was doing so well: bright eyed, lovely fur, full of life and then, suddenly, clearly unwell, lying in the litter tray, stone cold and screaming. It was rushed to the vet who put it on a heat pad and tried to find a vein to put fluids into it but the poor wee soul died. It had already had a blood test that showed it did not have feline aids or leukaemia but they said there was fluid around the chest and I have asked for a post mortem to be carried out so that we know what happened to it.

Whenever possible, all our animals are vaccinated by the time they leave here if they are the right age and we pride ourselves on how little illness we encounter with any of our animals. We have never had to close our cattery for an outbreak of cat influenza. We clean the floors with a very expensive disinfectant that is the one veterinary practices use; we change the bedding every day; and there is plenty of fresh air circulating and the feral cats have free access to the outside enclosure. The only time we had kennel cough in the kennel block was when it was undergoing renovation and the doors had been closed all the time, whereas normally doors and windows are continuously opening and closing and all the dogs are sent out into their outdoor run at intervals throughout the day.

We have had a couple more call-outs to deal with dogs in homes where officials need access. However, on both occasions it came to nothing because on one occasion there turned out to be no dog in the house and on the other occasion the eviction did not happen. Had it gone ahead, the three dogs in the home would have had to be taken somewhere. Folk that are financially stretched are unlikely to have their dogs vaccination and so boarding kennels will not take them, even if the owner could afford to pay, which they often cannot. Therefore, the dogs could have been brought back to MAA because their owner would have needed to get their own accommodation sorted before they could provide a home for their dogs. Even though we ended up with nothing to do but be present, we were paid, so that was good.

Currently in kennels we have a beautiful black Labrador whose owner has gone to prison, so who knows how long we will be housing the dog unless, of course, the owner gives permission for him to be rehomed. I will try to make contact with the owner to ask what he wants to do about his dog.

Poor Lucky, the Staffie who has been waiting so long for the court to determine his fate, has to wait even longer now because his owner failed to appear in court yet again. It is so unfair on this lovely-natured dog that has changed beyond recognition during his stay with us.

We are offering temporary housing to a cute wee pair of dogs, one being a black Chihuahua. Their owner has broken her wrist and will be collecting them as soon as she is able to manage them. On the same day, two Belgian Shepherds came in because of a tragedy in the family who need a bit of time to sort things out. The kennels were very full at this point and then two Cavalier King Charles Spaniels were picked up straying. This pair were microchipped but it had never been updated and so they had to wait until their concerned owner called us to see if they had been handed in. Fortunately, the home check was satisfactory and Annie, a gorgeous looking Saluki, went off to a new home, vacating her kennel. Annie has a lovely gentle nature although she has a shy disposition and lacks confidence. She lays in her bed looking up at people in a most seductive manner and when she is petted it is obvious that Annie has a lot of love to give. It is a good thing that she has gone because a couple who walk dogs here were breaking their hearts over Annie. This couple have, for years, taken on MAA dogs that needed fostering or 'temporary' care when recovering from a major operation. The dogs they take on end up staying forever with them. They have had very old dogs, three-legged dogs, and dogs with major health problems. Had Annie been here any longer I am sure she would have joined Nevis, the dog they currently care for, that has had major surgery on its leg and a series of operations on its eyes.

I have done a couple of talks to groups this week, something that is not my favourite activity because it makes me nervous. However, the talks went well and those who attended appeared to be really interested, asking questions that gave me an opportunity to explain more about how we work. It is easy to forget that what is obvious to us is a total mystery to other people and I try to do as much as I can to spread the word about our work.

Another opportunity to make us better known arose when we

were invited to attend an event at the Town Hall attended by companies and organisations who offer grants or advice on grant applications. We got some good advice about the kind of grant applications that are more likely to be successful. For example, if you want to get money for a particular project it is more likely to be successful than just looking for funding to help with running your charity. I am learning a lot more about the grant process than I ever knew and it was a really good use of time.

People do strange things and a family who won a quiz where the prize was a dozen fresh farm eggs, donated by us, put them in an incubator. Six cockerels and four hens was the result but they wanted MAA to take all but one of the cockerels and they would keep all the hens. Well, we certainly do not want any more cockerels because the ones we have already got all get along well but by introducing new ones we could end up with vicious fights. I asked what he planned to do if the cockerel and the hens they were keeping bred, which they would do, and who did he think would take another lot of cockerels. I also pointed out that he lived in the centre of a village and did he think his neighbours would appreciate the noise a cockerel makes very early in the morning? I also asked if he had thought about what chickens do to lawns and flower beds! I think this made him reconsider and so I am going to ask a friend who has plenty of space and might take some more cockerels to go over and see if she can help him out.

Not a good night for me when my friend was unable to help with the evening routine because she had visitors and Graham was desperate to watch a really important football match. So, that left me to do the evening cleaning and feeding in the kennel block, which was full, and all of the evening routine with the sheep and goats, cat litter trays and the chickens, the latter being one of the creatures I am allergic to. All the animals need fresh food and water at night and those we protect from nocturnal predators need to be shut in. This meant that by 10pm my eyes were red and itchy and my nose was streaming and I said a few uncharitable words to Graham! To crown it all, Moss, one of our Border Collies, managed to roll in something disgusting just before bed and so he was definitely not allowed to sleep on our bed. He hates a proper shower so I have used a dry shampoo on him but he is not sleeping with

Nevis with his lampshade and showing off his awards

us until that awful smell has completely disappeared. And, on top of all this, the computer has started to play up and I rely on this stupid machine. Fortunately, I managed to get the right person on the telephone from BT and he talked me through what was happening and how I could put it right - and it worked, so I am back in communication with the world.

Week 23

We have a total of five cat-catching boxes. Two are a bit flimsy but the other three will hold a very bad-tempered cat indeed. We also have two smaller boxes that can be placed at the end of the bigger boxes so that a very aggressive feral cat in need of urgent treatment can be taken to the vet and restrained whilst it is sedated or examined. We call them catching boxes because people do not like the sound of the word 'traps', although that is what they are and they are an important aid in bringing a cat, domestic or feral, to safety. It has taken us a long time to accumulate the catching equipment that we now have and they are all always out around the Highlands after folk report stray cats and kittens.

We are still trying to catch a stray cat around Fortrose Golf Course. It had been seen on a regular basis for weeks so we went along with the trap and left it with one of the staff, giving her instructions on how to set it during daytime but to shut it when she left work since it is far too cold to leave it out at night. The staff had not seen the cat for quite some time so it was possible that it had found a more lucrative place to stay because there are a lot of houses in the vicinity and during the summer months there is a campsite right beside the golf course. If it had found a cat-loving holidaymaker who was prepared to feed tasty delicacies to a poor pussycat, well, it might have been taken into their care and transported elsewhere. With this in mind, we collected the trap again because we needed it in order to try to catch the mother cat and her remaining kittens that were near Alcaig. That, of course, was the day the golf course stray was seen after an absence of weeks!

All we could do was set another trap at the roadside at Alcaig and keep going and checking it, along with a friend who lives close by. Unfortunately, we only managed to catch two of the kittens and this was just by Graham's speedy reactions rather than using the trap. The pair of them were so easy to tame down that they have already gone to new homes. The mother cat must be working so hard to feed her kittens and the food in the trap might attract her but we have to catch the other kittens first or they will die without their mother. We now need one of the boxes on site here since a tabby stray has been seen around, even sitting on the kennel block at night, activating the security lights.

We were called to a local town this week to pick up a cat whose owner has passed away. This poor creature had lost its home when the owner died and it was being fed by kind neighbours until we were able to collect it. They knew that with winter coming on it was no life for the creature. It was elderly and had so many health problems including a thyroid problem, a bad heart and terrible teeth and gums, the heart problem being so severe that its teeth could not be attended to. It would be really difficult to rehome it and the vet felt it was suffering, so the kindest thing to do was to put it to sleep and that was what we did. We cannot always have happy endings unfortunately. But, another elderly cat was handed in and it turned out to also have a thyroid problem, which is not unusual in a cat of this age. Fortunately, I found someone who would foster the cat with MAA funding the ongoing costs in relation to the thyroid problem.

I wonder how many people are living in terrible poverty but too embarrassed to ask for help. From time to time, we have a man contact us begging for food for his dog since he has no money to feed neither the dog nor himself. We have delivered food to him for the dog and, sometimes, from our own money and not MAA money, included food for him or money for the electric meter since the place is freezing cold. He does not seem to have an alcohol or drug problem but clearly has mental health issues and no idea how to manage what little he has. His dog looks clean and very happy and although the home is desperately in need of cleaning, there is no obvious dog poo around so the dog must go out. How many people in the UK exist like this and remain under the radar of social services?

We offer food to four food banks for recipients who have a pet but there is at least one food bank that refuses to take it because, they say, their purpose is to provide food for human beings and not animals.

We were given a couple of refrigerators and a cooker which is so fortunate since we were planning to buy a small fridge and cooker for use at the annual fete, the old ones being just about done in. The kind couple who donated them have a wonderful cat from MAA. He was in a dreadful state when he was handed in and to see him now you would not believe it is the same animal. The cat was actually passed on to us via a small local rescue centre that no longer exists. There is currently nothing to stop anyone setting up a rescue centre and there are many such places across the UK. Usually, they are started by well-intentioned animal lovers but they have not always thought through everything involved. Sometimes they are just folk who love animals and take more and more into their homes, not saying they are a rescue centre, but just enjoying having multiple dogs and/or cats around them. Then people hear that they will take unwanted animals and they feel sorry for the beast so just cannot say no or they find the animal dumped at their door.

If they are in an area where there are neighbours this frequently becomes a source of dispute and the individual or couple become isolated. They can become overwhelmed by the growing number of animals in their care with increasing food and veterinary bills until they become prohibitive. They may not realise the amount of time needed to look after the number of animals they have taken on and then, when they want to stop or become too unfit to struggle on, they have to find somewhere for all the animals to go to. We know of someone who has seventeen dogs at the moment and all kept outside in kennels, so this is an unusual way of keeping them as pets since contact must be limited. If someone registers as a charity they need to be prepared for all the paperwork that this involves, including setting up separate bank accounts and they need to be prepared for organisations such as the SSPCA, vets, police etc to visit their establishment.

We collected a Staffie we had rehomed nine months ago because he had apparently growled at one of the children who, according to the parents, could be rather boisterous! The dog is not that old, but it looks worn out, so I wonder how much peace it got? It has

Wonderful Rufus and Shona

gone out to a quieter home this time and one with no young children.

We are offering temporary accommodation to Rufus and Shona, two extremely overweight Border Collies, whilst their owner recovers following a fractured leg. They are a bit confused at present, which is understandable since they are not sure why they are here, but they are watching all the comings and goings with great interest. We have put down a couple of duvets in their shared pen so that they can sleep in comfort: their size would mean they needed enormous dog beds and they would be left with no room to move around. Our walkers love taking them out since they are content to plod along enjoying sniffs and I do not think they have ever had much walking before or, at least, not for quite a while. This pair are real characters and they always wag whenever anyone walks by.

Our own GSD puppy, Tara, has been in to be neutered. She is such a muppet that she tried to attack a large stuffed dog toy in the

149

waiting area and then a toy cat in the consultation room. This was useful because she was so fascinated by the cat that the vet was able to do the examination without having to struggle with this boisterous young lady. The neutering went well and she came out wearing a baby-grow affair to stop her touching her sutures and it worked really well. We are keeping her in a giant-sized dog pen for the time being to limit the amount of exercise because she is normally very, very active. Even whilst in the pen she is trying to chase the cats or play with the other dogs but I am limiting her to lead only exercise, separate from the other dogs, so she is not temped to thrash around with them as she normally does.

Sometimes I am a bit suspicious about whether an animal that is in a very poor condition has been picked up as a stray by the kind folk who bring it in or whether the truth is that they own the animal and have allowed it to get into a state that they are rightly ashamed of. They may see their only way of dealing with this situation that has got out of hand is to say they found it like this. Whichever is the case, the sooner an animal in need can be brought here and checked over by a vet the better. This puppy was, apparently, found in a layby not too far from here. The poor creature had a dreadful case of mange, which is a very painful, itchy soreness that, because they scratch to try to relieve the irritation, results in infections. It also had a hugely bloated stomach since it was full of worms and, as you can see from the photograph, it also had rickets. Something just was not right about the layby story and so I contacted the SSPCA who were going to check that there were no other puppies at the address the couple had given.

I have been meeting with someone from one of the local newspapers who is going to put our Christmas advert in. It is a chance to say a big, public, thank you to all the people who make donations and take cats and dogs from MAA. It also reminds people that we are continually in need and whatever donations they can make, no matter how small, are very gratefully received. Our collections during this run-up to Christmas usually do very well and there are some folk who wait to see our collection stall in one of our regular places so that they can contribute money they have been saving, in a jar for instance, throughout the year. Others come along with pre-written cheques and several people make signifi-

*Above: Worms,
rickets, fleas and
mange
Right: The same
puppy but looking
much better*

cant donations in lieu of buying Christmas presents for work col-
leagues or family. Our volunteers staffing the stall get to hear lots
of stories about animals folk have taken from MAA and what a difference, usually positive, the animal has made to their life. There is
one lady who tells them every year about how badly behaved her
sister's dog is and how she cannot understand why the sister loves
the animal and will not hear a word said against it.

Week 24

The hedgehogs are now in the cat house where we can contain the smaller ones but the big one, Pudding, can come and go as it pleases through the cat door and out into the outdoor enclosure. The underfloor heating in the isolation block was clearly not suiting them but trying to get them in the right temperature was really difficult and the only place we could think of was the cat house. By the spring time, the wee ones will be able to come and go as well. The cats will not interfere with them because of their prickles. Of course, hedgehogs may dig their way out from any enclosure but, hopefully, they might not because they have such a lot of space to wander around in safety and there is always food for them and the cats so why leave? It also means we can keep an eye on them should they get any health problems and come next year they will all be big enough to hibernate somewhere where they will not end up in a bonfire or run over. It has been a long haul feeding and cleaning them, particularly Hoggy because he was so tiny when he arrived, and coping with their smell is not for the faint hearted, but it will be wonderful to see them all living a natural life and finding somewhere nice to hibernate in winter 2020.

Two wee dogs that came in for temporary care whilst their owner recovered from a fracture have gone home. We had to drop them back at their home and I must admit I was very disappointed by the attitude of the owner who showed little reaction to the dogs and no gratitude at all for the fact they had been cared for. Maybe she thought we are council employees, paid to provide care at the request of the police or social services. We were not looking for a donation to cover their care, although anything would have been a welcome gesture, but a 'thank you' would have been nice. Thankfully, we see the other side of people who are grateful for

Time for breakfast

everything and anything MAA has done for their animal, even if it is just for a few hours when it has been brought in as a stray.

I have sent off a letter to the prison service addressed to the man who owns the gorgeous-natured black Labrador. In the letter I have explained that he is going to be in prison, we understand, for a year and it would really not be kind to keep the dog in the kennels for all that time. I do not know which prison he is in but I sent it to a central point and, having spoken to someone there, they have assured me that it will be passed on to the gentleman.

Blood samples from two of our kittens that look very much like wildcat hybrids have been sent off to Edinburgh Zoo. No results back yet because they apparently wait until they have a batch of these to do. The results will be very interesting since our expert at Aigas said that because they are ginger it is less likely that they have wildcat genes but the strange thing is that although ginger cats are usually males we have one male and the other is a female. These two not only have a lot of wildcat characteristics but they are very ferocious, even more than usual, and they were a real challenge to get hold of to take to the vet for neutering, which has now been done.

We are managing to get homes for a number of cats and kittens, making sure they are vaccinated if at all possible before they go, for flu, enteritis and leukaemia. I do not really like kittens to leave their mother until they are at least eight or nine weeks old but if they need to go earlier I make sure it is to a responsible home where they will be taken to the vet at the appropriate times.

Ninety per cent of the calls we get from people asking for a cat or kitten provide no details at all. It is important to be very careful who cats and kittens go to because it is not unheard of for people to get kittens to use for bait in dog fights or to sell them on for money. I want to know what experience the potential owners have had with cats in the past; how close they live to a busy road; who lives in the household; what other pets they have; and what they know about the feeding and treatment a kitten or cat would need. You might go into a shop and point to a loaf of bread and no questions asked but a kitten is a living creature and no matter how it annoys a potential cat owner, I will ask all these questions and they will not get a cat or kitten from here if the answers suggest it will not be a suitable home.

Charlie Drake the duck has got a limp again but it comes and then goes away. Whether this is just another part of the old injury that damaged his wing and prevents him from flying or whether it has something to do with frosty ground or stepping on something particular I really do not know, but it does not seem to stop him doing anything he wants. At 10pm one night, I discovered Charlie wandering around the car park when he should have gone to the shed for the night along with the other chickens. The last thing we do before taking our dogs for the night walk is to lock the hen houses and we always do a head count when we go to shut them in, so we would have noticed he was missing. Glen the goose also has a limp sometimes but that can be put down to his advanced years. We do not know how old Glen is but we do know that he has been here for twelve years.

A member of staff sustained a few bruises when she went into the field to recapture our two resident seagulls. Neither can fly and they live in an open-topped run with a shed at one end for their shelter. They had escaped when the door was left open for a moment and, for their own safety, had to be recovered quickly. The field is shared by Glen the Goose, numerous chickens, the goats and some of the sheep and it was one of the sheep that decided to repel the invader and head butted the poor lass back across the field and out. Sheep have very hard heads as this lass will testify!

Week 25

Just received a call from another organisation that deals with cats to tell me that they have received a call from a lady (no names, obviously) asking for a kitten. However, this same lady got rid of two older cats earlier in the year, saying she was allergic to them. It is unusual if she is suddenly not allergic to a new, younger cat! This sort of thing happens all the time. For example, people get rid of animals when they want to go away on holiday and the owner does not want to, or cannot, pay boarding fees. In this area, all the organisations dealing with animals know each other well enough to pass on relevant information, without breaching the Data Protection Act of course, because you can be taken in by people. People will tell the most amazing lies in order to get us to take an animal in. There is someone who contacted me earlier this year to take an old dog because she was dying with lung cancer and did not have long to live, but I know that she is not only still very much alive, and seemingly healthy, but she also has acquired a new dog! If she has had a miracle cure then I am really pleased for her but having done this job for so long, I have become a little sceptical.

A poor wee kitten was found stuck in a fence at Kinlochewe. It was definitely not feral and could have been dumped but it was a darling little thing. I put it in the shed in a separate crate along with all the other feral kittens in their crates. It was fine on Saturday morning but by the afternoon it started sneezing its head off and I was really concerned because I have been moaning about other organisations letting cat flu run rampant through their facilities and was this going to be a cat flu situation here? We isolated it as a precaution but it did not look like it was ill. Anyway, I rang the vet and got an appointment for that afternoon. The vet examined it and found it had a loose tooth and there was an infection there and, in response, the cat had been pawing at its face and had a cut just in its nose, which was making it sneeze. It had the tooth removed, some antibiotics and a couple of injections. No more sneezing and a big sigh of relief from us. Within two days it was off to a lovely new home by the seaside. We have done exceptionally well in getting cats and kittens away to new homes, but, my goodness, we needed to when you think back to how many kittens we have had to cope with in the last few months.

The reader may remember that we had been told about a mother cat and her kittens over at Alcaig but the person who owned the garden they had been seen going into would not allow us to set the cat trap to rescue them. We had a bit of good luck one day this week when someone rang to say that a cat with kittens had been coming into her garden this week and when I asked about catching them, she was only too happy to let us set up the traps in her garden so I really hope we can rescue them before the snow comes. We have to make sure we catch the kittens before the mother cat or they will die anyway.

We have quite a few animals handed over to us when their owner has passed away and none of their family feels able to take on their pet. This week we had another two gorgeous adult cats handed over by a woman whose husband had died. They had been his cats and she did not really like cats. These two cats had been together for seven years and although the woman said she could probably get a friend to take one of them, the other one would need to come here. I knew that I had someone on the lookout for a couple of adult cats and the woman agreed that it would be better for them to stay together. They had lovely characters and were rehomed that same day.

A pure white dove was brought in from Inverness because it had been hanging around for a few days. The kind gentleman laid a trail of food that led to his car and the dove obligingly hopped up and in. He then drove the bird here and when he arrived it was sitting contentedly on the back of his seat. We had it here for a couple of days and were pretty certain that there was nothing wrong with it so we released it. After taking a moment or two to orientate itself, it headed back in the direction of Inverness, so I reckon it will have gone back where it came from. The chap who brought it in wondered if it had been used as a dove that is released at a wedding because that is, apparently, a good luck thing to do and an increasingly popular thing. How the doves are caught, and whether they are tamed and released like a homing pigeon, I just do not know.

Graham has been spending time fixing up a shelter for the highland pony and his friend the donkey. The pair share a separate field from the other horses. The shelter already existed but had got into a bit of a state over the years and benefitted from a new roof so they are nice and dry and cosy for the winter. Rain and driving wind is hard on animals and all the horses have access to shelters and they can pick and choose who they share with.

Graham enjoys going to the auction mart and this time he went because there were a couple of tombstone feeders that we could use to provide the horses with hay, especially since we produced forty-five big round bales worth over £1,000. If we managed to get them we planned to create a canopy over them so that the hay would stay nice and dry, no matter what the weather threw at us. However, although they were really old and rusty, they went for nearly as much as new ones so that was out of the question. What he did buy were four tanks that we can use for water for the horses. We have a water trough in one of the paddocks but in the other the burn freezes in harsh winter weather and dries up if we ever get a good summer, so these will be a considerable asset to us. The first year we had horses here, I was a lot younger but I had to trek through thigh-deep snow carrying bales of hay and buckets of water along the track every day. We are still trying to find a tractor to replace the very old one we currently persuade to work but most of the ones for sale are out of our reach and there are not many for sale up here in the Highlands. There are quite a lot for sale down south and they are around £3,000 cheaper than any that are for sale up here.

We thought we might have found someone to rehome Rocky, our Anatolian Shepherd Dog who has been with us for so long. He has proved unsuccessful in a couple of homes, despite it being with experienced owners and so I asked one of our volunteers who knows Rocky well to contact the woman. This volunteer takes

Rocky out for long walks every day and sometimes off for trips in her car, so she really has a very good picture of Rocky. After their conversation the potential owner decided that Rocky was not really the dog for her but she was interested in another dog that she heard about and he would be ideal on the farm where she lives.

Tara is now on off-lead walks in the woods after her operation. She has inbuilt radar that can pick up anything that she could chase but, much to my relief, she completely missed a black-and-white cat that ran across the path and shot fifteen feet up a tree. I was so relieved that she had missed it since she would have been hurling herself around and attempting to climb the tree, which would have been a bit too early after her operation. I watched for a while, without making it obvious to Tara what I was doing, and was pleased to see that the cat came down when it was ready and quietly left the scene.

Graham and I had to make a trip over Balintore way to collect an unwanted kitten. This gave us the opportunity to call in for a cup of tea with a couple who have been amazing supporters of MAA for many years. They had lost their beloved dog and had told me they were never having another dog since they just could not go through that crippling grief again. They were very pleased to see us and invited us in straight away for a cuppa. It was at that point that I said we could not stay for too long because we had a wee doggy waiting outside in the car. I knew full well that they would say to bring her in and that was it – ten minutes later my devious nature was being commented on and the wee Yorkshire Terrier was happily established in its new home. Job done: sometimes, you just have to give things a little bit of a push!

It is amazing how you can get money from unexpected sources. I had collected some old bank notes that people have handed over after they have returned from holidays abroad and I managed to sell them to a company that provide cash for coins in exchange for £42. Now I am about to send off all the coins I have accumulated and get cash back for these, although I do not yet have a true idea of how much they are worth. Whatever it is, it is better than just having them sitting in a cupboard here.

A bit more money was made when we were invited to attend an event at Brodie Castle where a number of charities would have stalls and members of the public could find out about the charity from those staffing the stall. Unfortunately, the footfall was very disappointing on the day but, although it was a long day for the two volunteers who did it, they had taken along some handmade Christmas items and managed to make £28, which does not sound much but it all adds up.

We were given some extremely nice new items by a local shop and one of our volunteers set up a stall at a local farmer's market, managing to make over £100 during the 2.5-hour stint. It is quite difficult to judge what will and will not sell at the moment but so long as the initial outlay is not very much and we have someone who is willing to spend the time, sometimes in a very chilly hall or shopping mall, then whatever we make is all to the good.

A phone call this week reinforced the fact that we must keep on finding ways to make money. That call came from an eighty-six-year-old man whose companion dog, Holly, had developed an abscess and the vet had quoted £800 for the operation that had to be done by the end of the week. He had tried to get help from the People's Dispensary for Sick Animals (PDSA) who told him he was unfortunately not eligible for any help. I told him that I would think about it because it was an awful lot of money to be giving to one person but I would see what we could do.

The more I thought about it, the more I knew that we had to do something to help and the more determined I became that we must try to encourage other national organisations such as PDSA, Blue Cross and Dogs Trust to become more actively involved in helping Highlanders. I rang him back and said we would pay £500 towards the operation costs and the relief in his voice was so evident. I contacted the vet doing the operation and confirmed that the money would be found and the animal was booked in for Friday this week.

However, I could not stop worrying that we had depleted the funds so significantly in respect of one individual case so, just on the off-chance, I put out an appeal over the internet asking if anyone felt able to contribute any amount of money, no matter how small, towards this operation we would be most grateful. Within eighteen hours over £1,600 was pledged by people in the Highlands. A couple of newspapers picked up the story and someone even offered to pay the whole cost of the operation. People are surprised to discover how difficult it is for folk in the Highlands to get help from national organisations. Someone sent money specifically to the owner, via MAA, to buy a treat for himself and his dog when it was all over.

In this job, I frequently see how unkind or thoughtless people can be but something like the response to this appeal makes me realise that there are a lot of very kind caring folk. The rest of the appeal money has already been used to pay for another two operations for other animals.

Week 26

Even when I go into a garage to get petrol, I meet folk who know me from MAA. They all chat about the animals they have had from us and this week I met a chap who had within the last week taken a Belgian Shepherd Dog from us. He said she was settling in really well although she had given the kids a couple of nips just to put them in their place. She had also decided that she liked travelling in the back seat of his car, even uninvited, but he thought that was quite amusing so I think she has found a long-term home.

We have taken in two cats after their owner ended her life. They are beautiful cats but the family are in such a state of despair and confusion, as if they are stunned. They cannot cope with these two on top of everything else. It is a hellish experience for family and friends and has such a lasting impact. Animals can certainly pick up when humans are in distress and it must have an impact on them when they know their owner is really down. They will often sit beside you, put a paw on you or climb up on you as if to try and give a bit of comfort. However, these two cats will get homes quite easily if the family confirm they can be rehomed and it is possible they could even go this week, so they will not have to be here for long.

We spend a lot of money on heating, using both electricity and oil, so we try to reduce the number of separate sheds that we are using to house various cats, hedgehogs, rabbits and so on. Even the chickens have a heat lamp for when it gets really cold. Our monthly direct debit is £300 but when the electricity provider said it needed to go up to £380 we refused, saying we would reduce our usage rather than have almost an extra £100 going out each month. We have acquired a Smart Meter and we watch carefully what we are using, but there is no way that any animal here will be allowed to go cold. In fact, the kennel block, which is heated by a new £3,500 industrial oil boiler using a couple of hundred pounds oil per month, is, according to our dog walkers and visitors, probably one of the cosiest places in the Highlands to be on a cold day! Cold wet strays and poorly animals have to be kept warm.

A cat that looked like a skeleton was found just sitting at the side of the road by a member of the public. It did not seem to have been hit by a vehicle but it looked very old, neglected and distressed. It had pus coming out of its mouth and obviously a chronic ear problem. Surprisingly, it was microchipped, showing it was twenty years old and could be traced to an owner in Coventry, but the contact details had never been updated and the contact numbers were no longer active. It was a disgraceful case of neglect and the vet confirmed that it had serious renal failure amongst other things and the only kind thing to do was to put it to sleep. It must have been looked after twenty years ago because very few people microchipped their cats but what had been its fate since then and, particularly, in its latter years? Nobody has been in touch with us to see if their cat was handed in.

A stray Labrador was brought in to the kennels by the police very late one night this week, after we had gone to bed. He was a nice dog, well cared for and microchipped. However, it takes me so much time to get through to the microchip companies and to get them to release details of the animal's owner, despite MAA being a recognised rescue centre and microchipping centre, that I just settled the dog into a warm bed with food and water for the night. I have had long discussions with operators at these companies and end up being quoted the Data Protection Act and having to provide postcodes, pin numbers etc. I got so fed up one evening that I told the operator that it was fine not to give me the owner's information but she, on behalf of the microchip company, would need to contact them direct to say their dog had been found and where it was. She assured me that this was not part of their remit. My first task for the next day was to contact the microchip company and then the owner but the owner beat me to it and rang up to ask if we had a black Labrador handed in. They were pretty quick at getting up here to recover their pet and I was glad because he had barked quite a bit during the night.

A gentleman telephoned to say his sister's wee dog had been staying with him for a week but the door had been left open and it had disappeared. The dog was reported by a number of people as it ran up and down a main road and off down side roads and back, obviously crossing the road to do so. I put out a plea on Facebook asking folk to watch out for the dog and try to catch it or let us know where it was. I got a call from someone quite a way into the country around Loch Ussie who had seen the dog up there. She was happy to have the dog-catching box set up in their cart shed and we baited it with food. They agreed to monitor the box and, apparently, the SSPCA had also been up there trying to catch this dog. However, the dog did not appear until Graham and I bought a fish supper and took it up to Loch Ussie to use as bait in the trap, although the enticing smell resulted in it being one or two chips short by the time we got there! The next morning they phoned to say the dog was in the box and the fish supper was inside the dog. The wee dog had been on the loose from Monday to Friday morning and he was back home with his owner within an hour, but she was never going to let her brother look after him again! The smell of hot fish and chips is a lovely smell, even to me as a vegetarian, and hungry dogs and cats just cannot resist it.

Friends popped in to see us and while the woman and I were talking, Graham took the man into the kennel block. Next time we saw them they had a Collie with them. It had only been in a few hours but it had just got itself a lovely home. They had only had it for a couple of hours when they suspected it was deaf. The vet confirmed this and thought it had probably been deaf from birth. The previous people, who had it for six years, either did not realise or just chose not to mention it in case we would not take a deaf dog. The new owners are perfectly happy to keep it and it is already at home with their other dogs and pets including goats and horses. We have a wonderful photograph of it asleep beside its new master on the settee.

We agreed to drive the two, very large, Border Collies back to be reunited with their owner now she was sufficiently recovered from a fracture. It was a very long drive up to the north coast and both Graham and I were very sad when we finally left them since we had become very attached to them. We told their owner that if she ever found she could no longer manage them then we would take them back into MAA and find good homes for them, preferably together.

Sadly, one of our Shetland ponies died suddenly during the night. He had suffered badly from laminitus before he came here, so he had to be kept in a grass-free enclosure eating hay, carrots and a little horse feed to prevent a recurrence of the condition. There was no sign of any kicking or thrashing about and so we assume it was a heart attack and he just keeled over and died. Graham had the job of digging a very big hole away from any watercourse so we could bury him within the nice home he had ended his days in. My niece, who cares for the horses and loves every one of them, is very soft hearted and is so sad. Earlier this year, she had been looking after a bee that could not fly and was heartbroken when it passed away.

We are still trying to catch the mother cat and her kittens along between Alcaig and Corntown. We have got permission from a lady to set the catching boxes on her land. We go up there a couple of times a day, baiting the boxes. Some of the kittens may already have been lost to pine martins or foxes. The home owner is happy to put food out for the mother cat so we hope we will be successful before the worst of winter sets in.

We have been putting out a catching box, on and off now, for a long time up at a local golf course but the cat they think is a stray seems to disappear for long periods and even when some nice smelly tuna is in the trap this cat does not take the bait or else he just has somewhere else that he goes to. There is a campsite very close to the golf club but if someone had brought their cat on holiday, they are most likely the kind of people who would be looking for their cat and contacting all rescue charities and vets to try to get it back. We have a very good relationship with both the golf club and the campsite so they are all on the lookout for this cat. Someone put a very untrue post on the internet saying that MAA just were not interested in rescuing this poor cat but that is absolute rubbish and we have been trying for a very long time and will continue for as long as it is likely the cat is still there.

A chap phoned to say he would like us to take his two Rottweilers because he is moving away and cannot take the dogs with him, but he wanted us to drive a good many miles in order to collect them. Shortly afterwards, we got a call from someone on the island of Lewis who wanted to hand over a Border Collie that was no longer suited to the work and he too thought we would drive over to collect it. Neither of them seemed to consider the use of our time, particularly if the weather is bad, and the cost involved in driving to these locations to collect animals. In the end, I told the Collie's owner to ask for the local SSPCA officer to collect the dog and take it on the ferry as far as Ullapool where I would meet them. I very much suspect that the Rottweilers will be brought here by their owner before Christmas.

Week 27

We moved the cat-catching boxes at Alcaig and captured two kittens and a male cat, who we assume is the father. There have been no further sightings of any kittens so we think the four that we have now gathered are all that remain alive. Mother has avoided capture but the boxes are still there and baited and we are sure we will have her reunited with her kittens soon.

It has been a totally exhausting year and a very emotional year too. With so many young animals to care for all at the same time, there have been days when Graham and I have been drained. It has been a funny year this year in that things have been moving more quickly than usual and we are rehoming more dogs and cats more quickly. Nobody can believe we only have eight dogs in the kennels this week, five being long-stayers. It is at this time of the year that I have to spend time composing the Christmas Newsletter to keep all our wonderful supporters in touch with what has been happening and to write all the thank-you cards to all the folk who send in donations and to the shops that collect on our behalf. As well as this, I hand write the Christmas cards, so for this reason alone, the fewer animals requiring attention the better.

Jason is still with us. This dog has changed so much in the time we have had him and especially so since one of our experienced dog walkers has devoted so much time to him, giving him nearly three hours of walk each day, regardless of the weather. Sometimes he goes to the play park to run off his lead. When he arrived here he was just a dog who had been tied up, given little attention, no training and was very destructive. He had not been walked or played with. Since he has been here, everyone speaks to him, everyone gives him treats, nobody says a harsh word to him and he knows exactly what time his two meals a day are coming. Jason

166

Jason (left) enjoying a walk and Lucky discovers that even the bars taste nice at MAA.

has even had a much needed shower and a blow dry with a hairdryer. I am very hopeful that in 2020 Jason will get the home he deserves. It will be a home without young children since he is not used to them and needs to stay calm and not be wound up. He needs someone who can devote a lot of time and attention to him because he will benefit from training. Occasionally, he will pee in his pen when he gets over-excited but if he cannot get outside quickly when he needs it you cannot blame him.

Lucky, the dog that has been waiting to find out from the court if he has to be destroyed, has now been released and signed over to MAA so that he can be rehomed. This is a different animal from the one that came into here after he bit someone and his owner was being prosecuted. His pen has been the one with a constant view of the kitchen where everything goes on and there are constantly different people talking, laughing, moving around and generally interacting with each other and with him. Now, he is a sociable, friendly, tail-wagging dog. Even this week his tail is still wagging although he has been to the vet to be dressed! Lucky is a nice-natured dog and will get a good home in 2020.

Another dog, also awaiting a decision from the courts, has really settled now although it has taken her some time to do so. She is much less reserved and far more sociable; she watches everything going on and is always on the watch for anyone with a pocket full of treats. She is a big strong dog and walking her is reserved to just a few walkers who are not going to be pulled off their feet. Her owners love her and are desperate to have her back with them.

Speedy, our long-stay Lurcher will be here for a while yet. He goes out in his muzzle so that he cannot bite other dogs but he still gets so worked up by other dogs that he has been known to nip the person who is walking him when he is prevented from attacking the dog. Someone will come along who loves the breed and Speedy is an attractive animal so, one day, an experienced owner will take on the challenge of Speedy and turn his life around but I do not pretend it will be easy.

Rocky remains a problem. He is an absolute sweetheart when he is in the kennels. One of our young volunteers, who is hoping to go off to veterinary college, has fallen in love with this huge dog. He will react to certain people that he just takes a dislike to and these are usually men, but most folk he gets along with. He is walked by the same few walkers, partly because of his enormous size and strength. One lady walker takes him out for hours, walking miles with him, much of the time off his lead. It does not matter what he meets, be it person, dog or horse, because he ignores them and just continues on his walk. She takes him for rides in her car to the coast and adores him but she has another dog and Rocky and that dog do not get on. He has failed every rehoming opportunity because he just cannot fit in with a normal social domestic situation and he tries to dominate and take control. We need someone with an outdoor space and outdoor lifestyle and a love of this particular breed. We shall see what happens next year.

Lots of people have shown an interest in Cooper during the past two years but nobody has followed it up. He is a very pretty, young, exuberant dog but he is deaf and difficult to train. He sees this place as his home and, once again, it tends to be the same walkers who take him out or take him to the play park to run off lead. He does get overly excited when there are a lot of comings and goings around the kennels but when all the dogs have set up a barking chorus, he can still be sleeping soundly in his bed oblivious to what is going on. But when he wakes up and is raring to go, he gets so excited!

We have agreed to keep the Labrador whose owner is in prison until he is released next year. This is a lovely good-natured dog and the owner has had him from a tiny wee pup and, until his arrest, had never had even a night away from him. So, the Labrador is on an extended holiday until he can be reunited with his adoring owner.

The overweight Border Collies, Shona and Rufus, are back with us since their owner decided she was not yet fit and able enough to give them the exercise they needed. They endeared themselves to us by being overjoyed to see Graham and me when we arrived back up north to collect them. They returned happily into their kennel, and their duvets, and their routine including nice long walks. Despite the fact that they plod along contentedly, one of our regular walkers slipped on ice and the lead came off Shona whilst in the woods. Shona decided she did not want to go back on a lead but would walk along either behind or in front of the walker and nip smartly away every time she tried to put the lead over her head. It happens some times that a dog will get loose and so, once we receive the phone call from the walker we organise a recovery party consisting of me and Graham and whoever else happens to be around. We put Shona's male partner, Rufus, on a lead and took him into the woods as back-up. However, the minute Shona saw Graham, her new best friend, she bounded up to him and her walker slipped the lead on again. No harm done, but the walker, who had never had this happen before in the ten years she has been walking dogs at MAA, had nightmares about losing Shona. They have not yet formally been signed over for rehome but the time is coming when their owner will have to decide if she can or cannot cope with their needs in the futures, but they are happy here for the time being.

Minty, the really wild feral mother cat has tamed down so much that she is most likely being offered a home very shortly. She is staying in the reception cabin at present where there is a continual stream of people in and out, talking to her, handing her treats and playing with her cat toys. At one point, I did think she would have to end up in with our colonies of feral cats because she was very wild indeed but, although it has taken months and she still has a little bit of an edge to her, she is now due for a very happy life as a domestic cat in a home environment. It will have to be a home where they let her take her time settling in and do not try to immediately cuddle and kiss her.

The DNA results have not yet been reported by Edinburgh Zoo and these two kittens remain extremely ferocious, putting their ears flat, wrinkling their noses, opening their mouths (containing lots of sharp, pointy teeth) and spitting loudly. They were just that bit too old to easily tame. They show no signs at all as yet of wanting any contact with humans, so it will be interesting to see just how much wildcat genes are in them. My guess is that they will end up as permanent residents in the cat barns.

Our lovely new, second-hand, barn is still not up but, hopefully, if we get some decent weather in the spring, it will be up and ready to accommodate much of our aging machinery by next winter. We might even have raised enough money to go with the grant from Edna Smyllie Trust to buy a new, second-hand, tractor to go in the barn.

In the previous year, MAA rehomed 458 animals and spent in the region of £35,000 helping pet owners faced with veterinary expenses that were essential but unaffordable. We have been in contact with the PDSA to see if there is some way that they could help people in the Highlands. We hope to be able to come to some arrangement with them in the new year because there are so many people on very low income who cannot benefit from the PDSA Pet Care Scheme and, because of our geographic location, cannot use a PDSA Pet Hospital.

Postscript: February 2020

The mother cat from Alcaig has now been captured, has been neutered and is in the process of being tamed down for a potential home, so no more cold, hard winters for her.

Minty, who was so wild, is now enjoying her new life as a domestic cat in a loving home.

The Rottweilers were delivered by their owner before he went away and, after a very short stay in kennels, they have gone to new homes.

Rocky, the boisterous Anatolian Shepherd Dog, is going to a new home and, fingers and toes crossed, it will prove to be a forever home since it is with the walker who so loves him and she is having a special outdoor area prepared for him at her house.

Graham is happy because we have taken delivery of a 'new' second-hand tractor and it will help with lots of his outdoor tasks.

Lucky went out to a new home but it proved not to be successful. One member of the household was disabled and Lucky was just too excitable around the home. He is back in his kitchen pen, wagging his tail as usual and waiting for another offer.

Charlie Drake is now using a guinea pig run with a paddling pool in it because his 'pal', Glen the Goose, attacked and injured him. Charlie has taken to wandering around the car park most of the time because he adores attention from people. However, he is a bit slower than the chickens in getting out of the way when cars come in, especially if the driver does not expect to find so many chickens and a flightless duck in the car park so, for his own safety, we have decided to look for a new home for Charlie.

The weather continued to be awful with gale after gale and one night a tree came down across the fence in the feral cats' outside playground. Some of the cats got out but were recaptured quickly

171

but one black pussycat is still missing even though we have a trap out with tasty food in it. Hopefully, he will return to his pals at some point. The only other time a group of feral cats got out was when my niece, Iona, was about four years old: she had been given a row for something or other and so decided that she was leaving home but before she left she opened the door to the cat shed and let them all out. She really did get a good scolding for that!

Willie Gunn, our Honorary Treasurer, my friend Wendy Nganasurian and I met with three senior representatives from the PDSA. They visited MAA and we were able to make clear to them the challenges faced by pet owners in the Highlands. We now wait to see what comes of this meeting.

Acknowledgements

My thanks to all the animals and people who have inspired this account of life at Munlochy Animal Aid. Once again, my thanks to my friend Wendy Nganasurian for her help in writing this and to Russell Turner, publisher of Bassman Books.